# MIDDLE EASTERN BASICS

# MY COOKING CLASS

# MIDDLE EASTERN BASICS
## 70 RECIPES
## ILLUSTRATED STEP BY STEP

MARIANNE MAGNIER-MORENO
PHOTOGRAPHS BY FRÉDÉRIC LUCANO

\* \* \*

FIREFLY BOOKS

# A FIREFLY BOOK

Published by Firefly Books Ltd. 2010

Copyright © 2010 Marabout

First printing

**Publisher Cataloging-in-Publication Data (U.S.)**
Magnier-Moreno, Marianne.
   Middle Eastern basics : 70 recipes illustrated step by step / Marianne Magnier-Moreno; photographs by Frédéric Lucano.
[256] p. : col. photos. ;  cm.
Includes index.
ISBN-13: 978-1-55407-759-5 (pbk.)
ISBN-10: 1-55407-759-1 (pbk.)
1. Cookery, Middle Eastern.  I.  Lucano, Frédéric. II. Title.
641.5956 dc22   TX725.M628.M34  2010

**Library and Archives Canada Cataloguing in Publication**
Magnier-Moreno, Marianne
   Middle Eastern basics : 70 recipes illustrated step by step / Marianne
Magnier-Moreno.
Includes index.
ISBN-13: 978-1-55407-759-5 (pbk.)
ISBN-10: 1-55407-759-1 (pbk.)
   1. Cookery, Middle Eastern.  I. Title.
TX725.M628M33 2010        641.5956        C2010-901581-9

Published in the United States by
Firefly Books (U.S.) Inc.
P.O. Box 1338, Ellicott Station
Buffalo, New York 14205

Published in Canada by
Firefly Books Ltd.
66 Leek Crescent
Richmond Hill, Ontario L4B 1H1

Printed in China

# PREFACE

Middle Eastern cooking has a magical effect on me, plunging me into a world that I don't know but, nonetheless, a world from which I came.

My father was born in Cairo, but he and his family immigrated to France during his youth. On the banks of the Nile, I feel only a strange nostalgia that expresses itself, no doubt, in my strong interest in the cooking of this region.

I discovered Middle Eastern cooking in France, through my family's and my friends' cooking. The couscous that I tasted when I went to sleep over at the home of my Algerian childhood friend remains a point of reference for me. Ghorayebah — those butter cookies covered in sugar that melt in your mouth when you bite into them — were prepared by the women of my family, and my sister and I were crazy about them. As for our rice pudding, it was definitely "from here," but the touch of orange blossom water reminded us of our roots. And if sometimes the orange blossom water had been added too generously, the dessert was no longer from here nor there but simply soapy! I learned very early on to carefully measure waters and spices with a strong flavor.

In this book, I wanted to retranscribe as faithfully as possible the flavors of the dishes I have tasted during my travels, but, mostly, I wanted to bring back the cuisine prepared by those close to me with such passion — the cuisine that reminded them of another place and another life, most often that of their childhood. I also tried to make the recipes quicker to prepare while also using ingredients that are available in supermarkets, so there would be no need to go to specialized stores.

Middle Eastern cuisine is here understood in the sense of "Mediterranean Middle Eastern"; it's largely represented by recipes from Morocco, Tunisia, Algeria, Lebanon and Egypt, but I've also included dishes from Iran, Israel, Greece and Turkey. I hope that, among all of these, you'll find recipes that will carry you away!

Marianne Magnier-Moreno

✳ ✳ ✳

## DIPS & SPREADS

## BITES

## SALADS & VEGETABLES

# BABA GHANOUSH

**↠ YIELD: 4 SERVINGS • PREPARATION: 25 MINUTES • COOKING: 45 MINUTES • RESTING: 1 HOUR ↞**

3 eggplants
1 garlic clove
1 lemon
2 tablespoons (30 ml) tahini
Salt, to taste

**PRELIMINARY:**
Preheat the oven to 500°F (250°C). Poke a few holes in the eggplants using the tip of a knife. Place the eggplants on a baking sheet lined with aluminum foil.

**TIP:**
You can drizzle a little olive oil over the baba ghanoush just before serving.

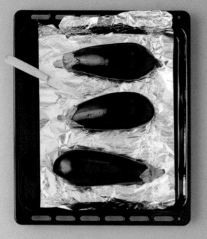

1 2
3 4

| 1 | Place the eggplants in the oven for 30 to 45 minutes. Turn them over halfway through the cooking process. They are soft when completely done. | 2 | Peel the garlic, remove and discard the germ and crush the clove with a mortar and pestle or finely chop it. Juice the lemon. |
|---|---|---|---|
| 3 | Holding the cooked eggplants by the stem, slice them lengthwise and remove the flesh using a spoon. Place in a strainer and mash with a fork, letting the juices drain. | 4 | In a food processor, blend the eggplant flesh and the rest of the ingredients using short pulses (the texture should not be completely smooth). Refrigerate for at least 1 hour before serving. |

# HUMMUS

➤ **YIELD: 1½ POUNDS (600 G)** • PREPARATION: 15 MINUTES • SOAKING: 12 HOURS • COOKING: 1 TO 3 HOURS ⬿

5 ounces (150 g) dried chickpeas
½ teaspoon (2 ml) baking soda
1 teaspoon (5 ml) salt
1 garlic clove

3 lemons (for 7 tablespoons/105 ml juice)
⅓ cup (75 ml) tahini
¼ cup (60 ml) olive oil

**PRELIMINARY:**
The day before, rinse the chickpeas and discard any that are spoiled or crushed. Soak them in plenty of water with the baking soda. Refrigerate overnight.

1  2
3  4

| 1 | Drain and rinse the reconstituted chickpeas, then place them in a saucepan. Cover with plenty of water and bring to a boil. | 2 | Cover and gently cook for 1 to 3 hours, depending on the type of chickpeas. Check doneness to ensure the chickpeas are cooked through. Season with salt and cook for an additional 5 minutes. | |
| --- | --- | --- | --- | --- |
| 3 | Peel the garlic, remove and discard the germ and very finely chop the clove. Juice the lemons. | 4 | Drain the chickpeas and reserve the water. Place all the ingredients, except the oil and chickpea cooking water, in a food processor. | ➤ |

Arrêt  Pulse

| 5 | Blend until creamy. Add a little of the chickpea cooking water to thin the hummus, if needed. | **TIP** ❋ <br> To obtain a really creamy hummus, it's important that the chickpeas be thoroughly cooked: they must be soft, almost pasty. |

| 6 | Serve the hummus in a dish and with a drizzle of olive oil on top. Enjoy with pitas. | **STORAGE**<br>❋<br>Hummus can be stored in the refrigerator for 2 days in a sealed container. Beyond that, the garlic taste will become increasingly more pronounced. |

# LABNEH

❖ **YIELD: 9 OUNCES (250 G)** • PREPARATION: 10 MINUTES • RESTING: 4 HOURS ❖

2¼ cups (560 ml) plain whole milk yogurt
½ teaspoon (2 ml) salt

| 1 2 |
| 3 4 |

| 1 | Mix the yogurt and salt in a bowl. | 2 | Line a strainer with a fine cloth or 2 layers of cheesecloth and place the strainer over a bowl. Pour the yogurt mixture into the center of the strainer. |
|---|---|---|---|
| 3 | Tie the cloth over the yogurt mixture by knotting diagonally opposite corners together. Refrigerate and let drain for at least 4 hours (the longer you let the yogurt drain, the firmer the labneh's texture will be). | 4 | Spread the labneh on bread, drizzle a little olive oil on top and finish with a pinch of the spice of your choice. Placed in a sealed container in the refrigerator, labneh can be stored for up to 8 days. |

# IRANIAN TZATZIKI

❧ **YIELD: 4 SERVINGS** • PREPARATION: 10 MINUTES • DRAINING: 10 MINUTES • RESTING: 1 HOUR ❧

½ cucumber
¾ teaspoon (4 ml) salt
10 mint leaves

1 small garlic clove
1 batch labneh (see recipe 3)
Pepper, to taste

| | | | | | |
|---|---|---|---|---|---|
| 1 | Peel the cucumber, seed it using a small spoon and finely grate it. | 2 | Place the cucumber in a fine-mesh strainer, season with the salt and let drain for 10 minutes. | 3 | Wash and dry the mint leaves. Stack them one on top of the other, roll them up and mince them. |
| 4 | Peel the garlic, remove and discard the germ and mince the clove. | 5 | Press the cucumber against the strainer mesh using a fork to squeeze out any excess liquid. | 6 | Mix the cucumber, mint, garlic and labneh in a bowl, season generously with pepper and refrigerate. |

# SPINACH DIP

➤ **YIELD: 4 SERVINGS** • PREPARATION: 20 MINUTES • COOKING: 25 MINUTES • RESTING: 15 MINUTES ◄

9 ounces (250 g) frozen chopped spinach,
  thawed
1 garlic clove
1 onion
1 tablespoon (15 ml) oil

1 pinch salt
1 teaspoon (5 ml) turmeric
1 batch labneh (see recipe 3)
½ teaspoon (2 ml) ground cinnamon

**PRELIMINARY:**
Drain the spinach in a strainer. Peel and
finely chop the garlic. Peel and mince the
onion.

1 2
3 4

| | | | |
|---|---|---|---|
| 1 | Heat the oil in a medium-sized skillet over medium heat, then add the onion and garlic and lightly brown for 10 minutes. | 2 | Put the spinach in a saucepan and add the salt. Cover and cook for 5 minutes over medium heat. |
| 3 | Add the turmeric to the onions and garlic and mix. Pour half of the onions and garlic into a small bowl. | 4 | Add the spinach to the remaining onions and garlic, and cook over medium heat for 10 minutes, uncovered, stirring regularly. ➤ |

| 5 | Transfer the spinach mixture to a bowl and chill. Add the labneh to the chilled spinach mixture and mix well. | **VARIATION**<br>❊<br>To speed things up, you can substitute Greek-style yogurt for the labneh. Take care, however, as the texture will be runnier. |
|---|---|---|

| 6 | Arrange the onions and garlic that you set aside on top of the spinach-labneh mixture. Refrigerate for at least 15 minutes. Sprinkle cinnamon overtop just before serving. | **OPTION**<br>❋<br>If using fresh spinach, you'll need about 1 pound (500 g). Wash it, remove any stems and chop it before cooking as indicated in step 2. Once the spinach is cooked, and before adding the onions, press it against the side of the saucepan to remove any excess liquid (discard the liquid). |
| --- | --- | --- |

# SEASONED FAVA BEANS

### ⟶ YIELD: 4 SERVINGS • PREPARATION: 20 MINUTES • COOKING: 40 MINUTES ⟵

3½ pounds (1.5 kg) fresh fava beans
½ teaspoon (2 ml) salt
1 garlic clove
1 lemon
¼ cup (60 ml) olive oil

**PRELIMINARY:**
Shell the fava beans and reserve one of the pods. Wash and drain the beans.

**TRADITIONAL RECIPE:**
Soak 7 ounces (200 g) dried fava beans in water with 1 teaspoon (5 ml) baking soda for 12 hours and cook as as indicated in step 2, but cook for 2 to 3 hours.

| | | | | | |
|---|---|---|---|---|---|
| 1 | Place the fava beans in a saucepan. Add the pod to enhance the beans' flavor. | 2 | Gently cook, covered, over low heat for 25 minutes: the bean's skin should not be hard when biting into it. | 3 | Crush 6 tablespoons (90 ml) fava beans with 3 tablespoons (45 ml) cooking water. |
| 4 | Add the crushed beans to the saucepan. Season with salt and simmer for 10 minutes, until the sauce is a little reduced. | 5 | Peel the garlic, remove and discard the germ and very finely chop the clove. Juice the lemon. | 6 | Serve the beans in bowls. Top each bowl with olive oil, garlic and lemon juice. Do not mix. |

# TARAMOSALATA

**❖ YIELD: 25 OUNCES (700 G) • PREPARATION: 15 MINUTES ❖**

4 ounces (120 g) white sandwich bread
  (3 or 4 slices)
7 tablespoons (105 ml) milk

7 ounces (200 g) tarama (cured cod or
  carp roe)
6 tablespoons (90 ml) lemon juice

1⅓ cups (325 ml) neutral oil (such as
  grapeseed, canola or sunflower)

1 2
3 4

| 1 | Remove and discard the crust from the bread and quickly dip the bread in the milk. Tightly squeeze the bread in your hands to remove any excess milk. | 2 | Place the tarama, the bread and the lemon juice in the bowl of a food processor. Blend until you obtain a paste. |
|---|---|---|---|
| 3 | With the food processor still running, drizzle in the oil. | 4 | Pour the taramosalata into a container, cover and set aside in the refrigerator until ready to serve. It's normal for taramosalata to become a little firmer once chilled. Serve on bread. |

# LAMB BRIOUATS (PASTRY TRIANGLES)

❖ **YIELD: 14 BRIOUATS** • **PREPARATION: 40 MINUTES** • **COOKING: 40 MINUTES** ❖

2 sprigs flat-leaf parsley
2½ tablespoons (37 ml) butter
½ onion
3½ ounces (100 g) leg of lamb, trimmed
3 tablespoons (45 ml) pine nuts

1 tablespoon (15 ml) olive oil
1 large pinch salt
Pepper, to taste
1 tablespoon (15 ml) plain yogurt
4 sheets brik or phyllo pastry

**PRELIMINARY:**
Preheat the oven to 400°F (200°C). Wash and dry the parsley, pluck the leaves from the stems and discard the stems. Coarsely slice the parsley leaves. Melt the butter.

8

| | | | | | |
|---|---|---|---|---|---|
| 1 | Peel the onion and mince. | 2 | Cut the meat into large pieces. Grind in a food processor. | 3 | Toast the pine nuts over medium-high heat until golden, stirring often. |
| 4 | Remove the pine nuts from the skillet and set aside. Add the olive oil to the skillet and brown the onion. | 5 | Add the lamb and toasted pine nuts. Lower the heat to medium-low. | 6 | Mix, breaking up the meat. Cook for 10 minutes, uncovered. ➤ |

7  8
9  10

| 7 | Take the skillet off the heat, season the filling with salt and pepper and add the yogurt and parsley. Mix and chill. | 8 | Stack the pastry sheets (without removing the parchment paper lining them). If the sheets are round, square them off. Cut the sheets into 4 rectangular strips. |
|---|---|---|---|
| 9 | Stack the strips one on top of the other. Take a sheet, peel off the parchment paper, brush the sheet with melted butter and place 1 heaping teaspoon (6 ml) filling at the edge. | 10 | Fold the pastry over the filling at a right angle, creating a triangle. Fold over again and flatten the filling a little. Continue to the end of the pastry strip and tuck in the end. Continue filling and folding pastry strips until all the filling is used. |

| 11 | Arrange the briouats on a baking sheet lined with parchment paper and bake for about 15 minutes, until golden. Serve hot. |
|---|---|

**EXPRESS VARIATION**

※

For a faster but heavier version, you can cook the briouats in a skillet. Heat 3 tablespoons (45 ml) oil and 1 tablespoon (15 ml) butter over high heat. Fry the briouats for 3 to 4 minutes, turning them over halfway through. Both sides should be crispy. Remove the briouats from the skillet with a skimmer or tongs and drain on paper towels.

# ZA'ATAR PITA BITES

❧ **YIELD: 24 BITES** • PREPARATION: 15 MINUTES • COOKING: 2 MINUTES ❧

6 pitas (homemade, see recipe 35,
  or store-bought)
6 to 7 tablespoons (90 to 105 ml) za'atar
  spice mixture
6 tablespoons (90 ml) olive oil

**PRELIMINARY:**
Preheat your oven's broiler. Line a baking
sheet with aluminum foil.

**TIP:**
You can also use the outer side of the pita,
in which case the result will be drier and
crispier.

1 2
3 4

| | | | |
|---|---|---|---|
| 1 | Using a pair of scissors, cut apart the two sides of the pita, reserving the thicker half. Arrange the pita halves with the inside facing up. | 2 | Put the za'atar in a small bowl, pour the olive oil on top and mix using a soup spoon. |
| 3 | Spread 1 or 2 tablespoons (15 to 30 ml) of the oil-za'atar mixture onto each pita half, distributing the mixture over the entire surface of the pita. | 4 | Cut each pita half into quarters and broil for 2 minutes, until the edges are golden. Serve immediately or at room temperature. |

# CHEESE & MINT CIGARS

➤ YIELD: 20 CIGARS • PREPARATION: 40 MINUTES • COOKING: 5 MINUTES ⬅

1 ounce (20 g) mint
5½ tablespoons (82 ml) butter
9 ounces (250 g) feta

1 egg, beaten
10 sheets brik or phyllo pastry
2 tablespoons (30 ml) olive oil

**PRELIMINARY:**
Wash and dry the mint, and pluck the leaves from the stems. Stack the leaves one on top of the other, roll them up tightly and mince.

1 2
3 4

| 1 | Melt ¼ cup (60 ml) butter in a small saucepan. Using a fork, mix the mint with the feta, then add the beaten egg. | 2 | Keeping the pastry sheets layered one on top of the other, slice them in half and, if the sheets are circular, square them off. |
|---|---|---|---|
| 3 | Brush a sheet with melted butter. Place 1 teaspoon (5 ml) filling in the center. Fold the long edges in by ½ inch (1 cm) and fold the sheet in half widthwise. Tightly roll up the sheet to form a cigar. Repeat to use up the rest of the pastry and filling. | 4 | Heat the oil and 1½ tablespoons (22 ml) butter in a skillet over high heat. Fry the cigars for 2 to 3 minutes, turning them over often, until crispy. Drain on paper towels, then serve. |

# FALAFELS

### ⇜ YIELD: 24 FALAFELS • PREPARATION: 25 MINUTES • COOKING: 6 MINUTES ⇝

4½ ounces (125 g) dried chickpeas
1 teaspoon (5 ml) baking soda
¼ ounce (6 g) cilantro
¼ ounce (6 g) flat-leaf parsley
1 small leek
1 garlic clove

½ zucchini
¼ teaspoon (1 ml) ground pepper
¼ teaspoon (1 ml) ground cinnamon
½ teaspoon (2 ml) ground coriander
1 teaspoon (5 ml) salt
Oil, for frying

**PRELIMINARY:**
The day before, rinse the chickpeas and
discard any that are spoiled or crushed.
Soak them in plenty of water with
½ teaspoon (2 ml) baking soda. Refrigerate
overnight.

1 2
3 4

| 1 | Wash and dry the cilantro and parsley, and pluck the leaves from the stems. | 2 | Discard the outside layer and the green part of the leek. Clean the leek and roughly chop it. | |
| 3 | Peel the garlic. Wash and roughly chop the zucchini. | 4 | Drain the chickpeas and blend in a food processor with the vegetables and herbs. Blend until you obtain a pasty texture. | ➤ |

5 6
7 8

| 5 | Pour the mixture onto a work surface and add the pepper, cinnamon, coriander, salt and ½ teaspoon (2 ml) baking soda. | 6 | Knead until you obtain a firm, uniform dough, about 1 to 2 minutes. |
|---|---|---|---|
| 7 | Divide the dough into 25 pieces and shape into balls using damp hands. | 8 | Heat the oil in a large skillet. Fry the balls for 6 minutes. |

| 9 | Remove the falafels using a skimmer and drain on paper towels. Serve hot. | **ACCOMPANIMENT**<br>❋<br>Falafels can be enjoyed with tarator sauce; made from roasted sesame seeds and lemon (see recipe 29). |
|---|---|---|

# FALAFEL SANDWICHES

### ❧ YIELD: 4 SANDWICHES • PREPARATION: 15 MINUTES ❧

25 falafels (see recipe 11)
½ ounce (12 g) mint
½ ounce (12 g) flat-leaf parsley
10 cherry or grape tomatoes

10½ ounces (300 g) radishes (1 bunch)
4 pitas (homemade, see recipe 35,
  or store-bought)
½ cup (125 ml) tarator sauce (see recipe 29)

**PRELIMINARY:**
Reheat the falafels in a skillet or in a 400°F
(200°C) oven for a few minutes.

| | 1 | 2 |
| | 3 | 4 |

| 1 | Wash and dry the mint and parsley, and pluck the leaves from the stem and coarsely chop the leaves. | 2 | Wash the tomatoes and cut into quarters. Cut off and discard the radish tops, wash the radishes and slice each into 3 or 4 rounds. |
|---|---|---|---|
| 3 | Using a serrated knife, slit the pitas open without completely separating them. | 4 | Mix the raw vegetables and herbs. Fill the pitas by alternating layers of vegetables and falafels. Add 2 tablespoons (30 ml) tarator sauce to each pita. |

# TUNISIAN SANDWICHES

❧ YIELD: 4 SANDWICHES • PREPARATION: 10 MINUTES ❧

2 (4-ounce/115 g) cans sardines in oil
½ teaspoon (2 ml) harissa
16 oven-roasted tomato petals with their oil
   (see recipe 20)

4 pitas (homemade, see recipe 35,
   or store-bought)
½ lemon, juiced
Salt & pepper, to taste

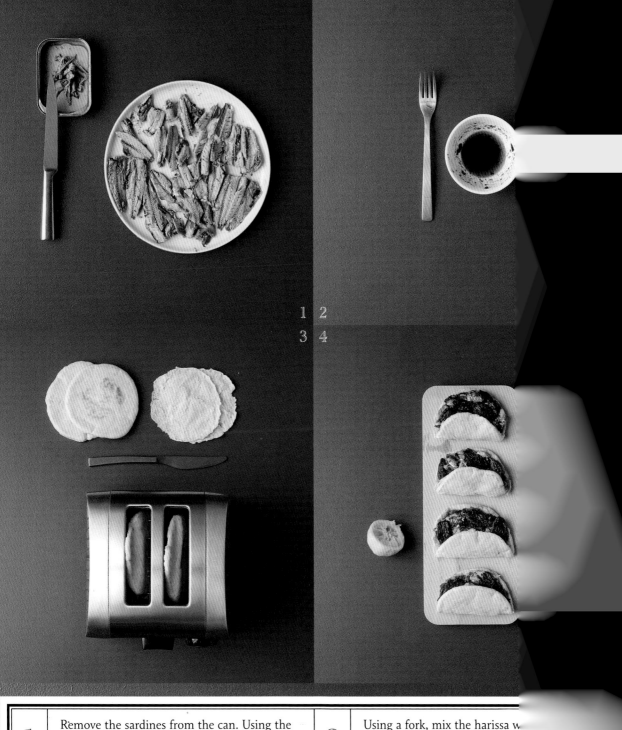

| | | | |
|---|---|---|---|
| 1 | Remove the sardines from the can. Using the tip of a knife, cut open the sardines and remove the spine. | 2 | Using a fork, mix the harissa w... spoons (30 ml) oil taken from... roasted tomatoes. |
| 3 | Toast the pitas in a toaster. Using a serrated knife, cut apart the two sides of the pitas and reserve the thickest part only. | 4 | Distribute the sardines over the... place 4 tomato petals on each... little oil-harissa mixture on eac... little lemon juice on top. Seaso... pepper and serve. |

# TABBOULEH

⤜ YIELD: 6 SERVINGS • PREPARATION: 30 MINUTES • RESTING: 1 HOUR ⤛

8½ ounces (240 g) flat-leaf parsley
1½ ounces (40 g) mint
4 lemons (for ⅔ cup/150 ml juice)
3 green onions, preferably large and mature
3 tomatoes

2 tablespoons (30 ml) fine bulgur
7 tablespoons (105 ml) olive oil
1 teaspoon (5 ml) salt

**PRELIMINARY:**
Wash the parsley and mint. Dry the mint and pluck the leaves from the stems. Gather the parsley into an organized bunch, and cut off and discard the stems. Juice the lemons.

1 2
3 4

| | | | |
|---|---|---|---|
| 1 | Finely mince the parsley leaves. Stack the mint leaves one on top of the other, tightly roll them up and mince more coarsely than the parsley. | 2 | Finely slice the green onions. Seed the tomatoes and finely dice them. |
| 3 | Place the bulgur, tomatoes, onions, herbs, lemon juice, olive oil and salt in a bowl. Mix thoroughly. | 4 | Cover and chill in the refrigerator for at least 1 hour before serving. |

# FATTOUSH

### ❧ YIELD: 4 SERVINGS • PREPARATION: 15 MINUTES • COOKING: 10 MINUTES ❧

5 ounces (150 g) radishes
3 green onions, preferably large and mature
2 pitas (homemade, see recipe 35,
  or store-bought)
½ ounce (15 g) mint
1 ounce (30 g) flat-leaf parsley

5 ounces (150 g) cherry or grape tomatoes
½ cucumber
1 Little Gem lettuce (or Romaine hearts)
7 tablespoons (105 ml) olive oil
2 heaping teaspoons (12 ml) ground sumac
2 tablespoons (30 ml) red wine vinegar

Salt, to taste
**PRELIMINARY:**
Preheat the oven to 300°F (150°C). Wash
and dry the vegetables and herbs. Remove
and discard the radishes' stems and cut off
the onions' stalks.

1 2
3 4

| 1 | Cut the pitas into small squares using scissors and then separate the two sides. Arrange the pita halves on a baking sheet and bake for 10 minutes. | 2 | Pluck the mint and parsley leaves from the stems. Cut the tomatoes in half, the radishes into fifths and the onions into thin rounds. Cut the cucumber in half lengthwise and then slice it. Slice the lettuce into strips. |
|---|---|---|---|
| 3 | Mix the olive oil with 1 heaping teaspoon (6 ml) sumac and coat the crispy pitas in the mixture. | 4 | Toss the ingredients together with the vinegar and salt, sprinkle 1 heaping teaspoon (6 ml) sumac on top and serve immediately. |

# ARUGULA WITH OLIVES

❧ **YIELD: 4 SERVINGS** • **PREPARATION: 15 MINUTES** ❧

7 ounces (200 g) arugula
5 ounces (140 g) black olives
4 green onions, preferably large and mature

2 lemons
¼ cup (60 ml) olive oil
Salt & pepper, to taste

**NOTE:**
You can use olives that are already pitted,
but they are generally not as good.

1 2
3 4

| 1 | Wash and dry the arugula. Pit the olives. Chop off and discard the green stalks from the onions and mince the bulbs. | 2 | Cut the ends off the lemons and peel them using a very sharp knife to expose the flesh. |
|---|---|---|---|
| 3 | Finely slice the lemons and then cut each slice into quarters or sixths, if possible. | 4 | Place everything in a salad bowl and add the olive oil. Season generously with salt and pepper. Toss and serve. |

# GREEK SALAD

❧ YIELD: 6 SERVINGS • PREPARATION: 25 MINUTES ❧

1 iceberg lettuce
1 green, red or yellow bell pepper
8 cherry or grape tomatoes
8 radishes
1 red onion
3½ ounces (100 g) feta

1 garlic clove
8 black olives
1 heaping teaspoon (6 ml) dried oregano
2 tablespoons (30 ml) lemon juice
½ teaspoon (2 ml) salt
½ teaspoon (2 ml) pepper

7 tablespoons (105 ml) olive oil
**PRELIMINARY:**
Wash and dry the lettuce. Wash the bell pepper, tomatoes and radishes. Peel the onion.

1 2
3 4

| 1 | Stack the lettuce leaves, roll them up and slice. Cut the feta into little pieces and the tomatoes in half. Slice the radishes, onion and bell pepper. | 2 | Peel the garlic, slice in half and lightly smash it with the side of a knife. Rub the smashed garlic against the inside of a salad bowl, then discard the garlic. |
|---|---|---|---|
| 3 | Place the vegetables, feta, olives and oregano in the salad bowl. Add the lemon juice, salt and pepper. Toss carefully. | 4 | Add the oil and toss again. Serve immediately. |

# MECHOUIA SALAD

**❧ YIELD: 4 SERVINGS • PREPARATION: 15 MINUTES • COOKING: 30 MINUTES ❧**

1 garlic clove
½ lemon
6 tomatoes
1 red bell pepper
1 yellow bell pepper
1 teaspoon (5 ml) capers

3 tablespoons (45 ml) olive oil
2 cilantro sprigs, washed & dried
1 tablespoon (15 ml) red wine vinegar
1 large pinch salt
Pepper, to taste

**PRELIMINARY:**
Preheat your oven's broiler. Peel the garlic, remove and discard the germ and finely chop the clove. Juice the lemon. Cover an oven rack with aluminum foil.

| 1 | Place the tomatoes and bell peppers on the rack. Grill the tomatoes for 5 minutes (until the skins split) and the bell peppers for 30 minutes (until the skins turn black), turning them over regularly. | 2 | Peel the tomatoes, remove the cores, slice them into eighths and seed. Let the bell peppers cool and then peel them, slice them in half, remove and discard the seeds and white membrane and slice them into strips. |
|---|---|---|---|
| 3 | Put the tomatoes, bell peppers, capers, garlic, olive oil and lemon juice in a salad bowl. Toss carefully. Let chill in the refrigerator. | 4 | Just before serving, pluck the cilantro leaves from the stems. Coarsely slice the leaves and add to the vegetables along with the vinegar. Season with salt and pepper and toss. Serve. |

# TOMATO & ONION SALAD

❖ **YIELD: 4 SERVINGS** • PREPARATION: 15 MINUTES • RESTING: 1 HOUR ❖

1 onion
4 tomatoes
2 tablespoons (30 ml) red wine vinegar
1 teaspoon (5 ml) salt

Pepper, to taste
¼ cup (60 ml) neutral oil (such as
   grapeseed, canola or sunflower)

1 2
3 4

| 1 | Peel the onion, slice in half and then mince. Wash the tomatoes, cut into quarters, seed and then finely dice. | 2 | Pour the vinegar into a small salad bowl. Add the salt and pepper and mix to dissolve the salt. |
| 3 | Add the oil and mix. | 4 | Add the tomatoes and onions, then toss well. Cover and chill in the refrigerator for at least 1 hour before serving. |

# OVEN-ROASTED TOMATO PETALS

❖ **YIELD: 32 PETALS** • PREPARATION: 15 MINUTES • COOKING: 3½ HOURS TO 4½ HOURS ❖

4 garlic cloves
2¼ pounds (1 kg) tomatoes on the vine
½ cup (125 ml) olive oil, plus extra to cover
   the jarred petals
1 tablespoon (15 ml) sugar

1 teaspoon (5 ml) salt
Pepper, to taste
1 teaspoon (5 ml) dried herbes de Provence
   or 3 to 4 sprigs fresh thyme

**PRELIMINARY:**
Preheat the oven to 210°F (105°C). Line a
baking sheet with parchment paper.

1 2
3 4

| 1 | Peel and smash the garlic cloves with the side of a knife without completely flattening them. Peel the tomatoes, cut into quarters and seed. | 2 | Mix the oil, sugar, salt and pepper with the tomatoes. |
|---|---|---|---|
| 3 | Spread out the seeded tomato quarters, peel side down, on the baking sheet. Distribute the garlic cloves between the tomatoes. Sprinkle the herbes de Provence on top. Bake for 3½ to 4½ hours. | 4 | Let cool. Place the tomato petals in a glass jar or plastic container. Cover with oil, seal and set aside in the refrigerator. |

# CHAKCHOUKA RAGOUT

❖ YIELD: 2 SERVINGS • PREPARATION: 20 MINUTES • COOKING: 1 HOUR, 5 MINUTES ❖

2 garlic cloves
1 onion
3 tablespoons (45 ml) olive oil
3 fresh tomatoes
1 red bell pepper

1 yellow bell pepper
3 oven-roasted tomato petals (see recipe 20)
1 teaspoon (5 ml) coriander seeds
1 pinch saffron

1 large pinch salt
Freshly ground pepper, to taste

1 2
3 4

| | | | |
|---|---|---|---|
| 1 | Peel the garlic, remove and discard the germs and smash the cloves with the side of a knife. Peel the onion, slice it in half and separate the "petals." | 2 | In a large skillet, heat 2 tablespoons (30 ml) oil over medium heat. Lightly fry the onion and garlic for 10 minutes, without browning, over medium-low heat. |
| 3 | Meanwhile, peel the fresh tomatoes (using a peeler for soft fruits and vegetables), cut into quarters and seed. | 4 | Cut off the ends of the bell peppers and slice them in half. Remove and discard the seeds and the white membrane. Slice the bell peppers into strips. ➤ |

| 5 | Add the fresh tomatoes and bell peppers to the skillet. Cook for 10 minutes over medium heat, stirring regularly. | 6 | Cut the oven-roasted tomato petals in half. |
|---|---|---|---|
| 7 | Crush the coriander seeds with a mortar and pestle. | 8 | Add the oven-roasted tomatoes, coriander seed, saffron salt and pepper to the bell pepper mixture. Mix well. |

9 | Cover and cook over low heat for 40 minutes, stirring occasionally. Cook for 5 minutes uncovered. Sprinkle 1 tablespoon (15 ml) olive oil on top and serve.

**TIP**
※

☛ If you don't have a mortar and pestle, you can instead put a few coriander seeds in a skillet and crush them with the bottom of a saucepan that's a little smaller than the skillet.

# SLATA JIDA

❖ YIELD: 4 SERVINGS • PREPARATION: 20 MINUTES • RESTING: 1 HOUR ❖

2 tomatoes
½ cucumber
½ red bell pepper
½ green bell pepper
4 green onions, preferably large and mature

½ ounce (15 g) flat-leaf parsley, washed & dried
1 lemon
1 tablespoon (15 ml) olive oil
2 pinches salt

Pepper, to taste

**PRELIMINARY:**
Rinse all the vegetables but don't peel them.

1 2
3 4

| | | | |
|---|---|---|---|
| 1 | Seed the tomatoes and cucumber. Seed the bell peppers and remove the white membrane and stems. Chop off any though stalks on the green onions. Pluck the parsley leaves from the stems and mince the leaves. | 2 | Slice the green part of the green onions into rounds and the white part first into quarters, then into slices. Finely dice the other vegetables (into about ¼-inch/5 mm cubes). |
| 3 | Zest and juice the lemon. | 4 | Sprinkle the lemon juice and oil onto the raw vegetables, add the zest, salt, pepper and parsley and mix well. Refrigerate for at least 1 hour before serving. |

2

## SOUPS

## SAUCES

# LENTIL SOUP

➤ YIELD: 4 SERVINGS • PREPARATION: 15 MINUTES • COOKING: 25 MINUTES ◆

9 ounces (250 g) dried green lentils
1 onion
2 tablespoons (30 ml) butter

4 cups (1 L) poultry stock, preferably
   chicken (or 1 chicken bouillon cube)
2 cinnamon sticks

1 teaspoon (5 ml) salt
Pepper, to taste

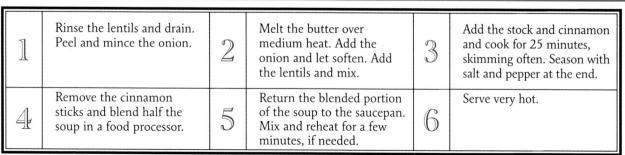

| 1 | Rinse the lentils and drain. Peel and mince the onion. | 2 | Melt the butter over medium heat. Add the onion and let soften. Add the lentils and mix. | 3 | Add the stock and cinnamon and cook for 25 minutes, skimming often. Season with salt and pepper at the end. |
| 4 | Remove the cinnamon sticks and blend half the soup in a food processor. | 5 | Return the blended portion of the soup to the saucepan. Mix and reheat for a few minutes, if needed. | 6 | Serve very hot. |

# CHICKEN NOODLE SOUP

➤ YIELD: 4 SERVINGS • PREPARATION: 40 MINUTES • COOKING: 55 MINUTES ➤

2 onions
2 tablespoons (30 ml) oil
2 chicken legs & 2 chicken breasts
5¼ cups (1.25 L) water
2 teaspoons (10 ml) + 1 pinch salt

1 bay leaf
½ carrot
1 celery stalk
⅓ ounce (10 g) parsley
½ lemon

3½ ounces (100 g) vermicelli noodles
Pepper, to taste

**PRELIMINARY:**
Peel and mince the onions.

| | | | | | |
|---|---|---|---|---|---|
| 1 | Heat the oil over medium-high heat and brown the chicken legs. | 2 | Remove the chicken from the skillet and set aside. Place half the onions in the skillet and let soften. | 3 | Return the legs to the pan, cover and cook for 20 minutes over low heat. |
| 4 | Add the water, 2 teaspoons (10 ml) salt and the bay leaf. Loosen any bits stuck to the bottom of the skillet using a spatula. Bring to a boil. | 5 | Add the chicken breasts and simmer for 20 minutes. Remove the breasts and set aside to cool. | 6 | Remove the legs and strain the stock. Let rest for 10 minutes (so the fat rises to the surface). ➢ |

7 8
9 10

| | | | |
|---|---|---|---|
| 7 | Meanwhile, peel the carrot and slice it in half lengthwise, and then slice both pieces lengthwise. Thinly slice. Thinly slice the celery stalk. | 8 | Remove the fat from the stock using a soup spoon and reserve about 2 tablespoons (30 ml) fat for cooking the vegetables for the soup. |
| 9 | Heat the fat over medium-high heat in the same skillet that you used to cook the chicken. | 10 | Add the carrot, celery, the rest of the onion and 1 pinch salt. Let soften for a few minutes, stirring. Do not let brown. |

| | | **NOTE** |
|---|---|---|
| 11 | Add the stock (and any juice in the container holding the chicken breasts) and simmer for 15 minutes. | ☞ Chicken legs are used to flavor the stock, but you don't keep them in the soup. Set aside in the refrigerator for later use. |

12 13
14 15

| 12 | Meanwhile, shred the chicken breasts into bite-size pieces using your fingers. | 13 | Rinse and dry the parsley. Pluck the leaves from the stems, discard the stems and mince the leaves. Juice the lemon. |
|---|---|---|---|
| 14 | Add the chicken breast meat to the soup and cook for 5 minutes. | 15 | After 5 minutes, bring the soup to a boil, add the noodles and cook for another 5 minutes. |

| | | **VARIATION** |
|---|---|---|
| 16 | Remove the saucepan from the heat, add the lemon juice, season with pepper and mix. Sprinkle the chopped parsley on top, then serve. | You can substitute small pasta, fresh or dried, for the noodles. You'll have to adjust the cooking time. |

# TOMATO & GARLIC SOUP

➤ YIELD: 4 SERVINGS • PREPARATION: 15 MINUTES • COOKING: 35 MINUTES ➤

1 onion
4 garlic cloves
3 tablespoons (45 ml) olive oil
½ teaspoon (2 ml) paprika
2 tablespoons (30 ml) tomato paste

⅓ cup (75 ml) tomato puree
3¼ cups (810 ml) water
1 heaping teaspoon (6 ml) salt
3½ ounces (100 g) vermicelli noodles
Pepper, to taste

**TIP:**
If desired, you can add 1 teaspoon (5 ml)
aniseed 5 minutes before cooking is done.

| 1 | Peel and mince the onion. Peel the garlic, remove and discard the germs and crush the cloves. | 2 | Heat the oil over medium-high heat. Add the onion, let soften, add the garlic and cook for 30 seconds. | 3 | Add the paprika, tomato paste and tomato puree. Mix. |
|---|---|---|---|---|---|
| 4 | Add 1 cup (250 ml) water and the salt, cover and cook over low heat for 15 minutes. | 5 | Add 2¼ cups (560 ml) water, bring to a boil and add the noodles. When the mixture boils, cover the pot. | 6 | Cook for 15 minutes over low heat. Season with pepper, then serve. |

# HARIRA

### ❧ YIELD: 6 TO 8 SERVINGS • PREPARATION: 35 MINUTES • COOKING: 1 HOUR, 15 MINUTES ❧

3 quarts (3 L) poultry stock (or 5 chicken
  bouillon cubes)
3½ ounces (100 g) dried yellow lentils
4 tomatoes (or 1 tablespoon/15 ml tomato
  paste)
2 onions
3 celery stalks

1 lemon
14 ounces (400 g) leg of lamb
2 tablespoons (30 ml) olive oil
1 teaspoon (5 ml) ground cinnamon
1 pinch saffron
7 ounces (200 g) cooked chickpeas, drained
  and rinsed

2 sprigs parsley
1 sprig cilantro
Pepper, to taste

**PRELIMINARY:** Bring the stock to a
simmer. Rinse the lentils. Peel the tomatoes
and onions.

1 2
3 4

| | | | |
|---|---|---|---|
| 1 | Cut the tomatoes into quarters and seed and dice them. Mince the onions. Rinse the celery, cut in half lengthwise and slice. Zest the lemon. | 2 | Dice the lamb (about ¾-inch/2 cm cubes). |
| 3 | Heat the olive oil in a sauté pan or skillet over medium-high heat. Brown the lamb on all sides. | 4 | Add the onions and celery, then fry for 2 to 3 minutes, until golden. Mix well. ➤ |

5 6
7 8

| 5 | Add the tomatoes (or the tomato paste), lemon zest and cinnamon. Mix. | 6 | Add the simmering stock, saffron and lentils. Bring to a boil, then cook, uncovered, for 1 hour over medium heat. Skim. |
|---|---|---|---|
| 7 | Five minutes before the cooking is done, add the chickpeas. | 8 | Wash and dry the parsley and cilantro. Cut off and discard the stems and mince the leaves. |

| | |
|---|---|
| **9**   Just before serving, season with pepper (if desired) and sprinkle the herbs on top. | **NOTE** ❊ |
| | ☛ If you don't have good saffron available, you can season this soup with 1 teaspoon (5 ml) ground ginger, adding it at the same time as the cinnamon. |
| **SERVING SUGGESTION** ❊ | |
| The soup can be served thickened. Mix ⅓ cup (75 ml) cornstarch with ¼ cup (60 ml) cold water just before serving. Add it to the soup and mix until it thickens. | |

# TAHINI SOUP

➤ **YIELD: 4 SERVINGS** • **PREPARATION: 10 MINUTES** • **COOKING: 25 MINUTES** ➤

5½ cups (1.375 L) water
1½ teaspoons (7 ml) coarse salt
½ cup (125 ml) long-grain rice (preferably basmati)

⅓ cup (75 ml) tahini
3 tablespoons (45 ml) lemon juice

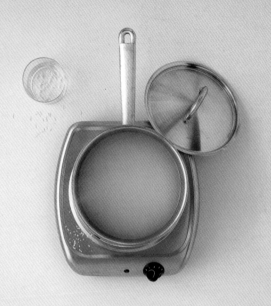

1 2
3 4

| | | | |
|---|---|---|---|
| 1 | Bring 5¼ cups (1.3 L) water to a boil. Season with salt and add the rice. Cover, lower the heat to low and cook for 20 minutes. | 2 | Meanwhile, whisk the tahini with ¼ cup (60 ml) water in a medium-sized bowl until smooth. |
| 3 | Add the lemon juice and mix well. Whisk 1 ladleful of rice cooking water into the tahini-lemon mixture. | 4 | Take the rice off the heat and add the tahini-lemon mixture to the saucepan. Mix, then serve. |

# EGGPLANT KHORESH

❧ **YIELD: 4 SERVINGS** • PREPARATION: 40 MINUTES • COOKING: 1 HOUR, 25 MINUTES ❧

2 onions
2 garlic cloves
1 pound (500 g) chicken breasts
3 tablespoons (45 ml) oil + about 1 cup
(250 ml), for frying

1 teaspoon (5 ml) turmeric
Pepper, to taste
2 cups (500 ml) tomato puree
2 eggplants
2 egg whites

1½ teaspoons (7 ml) salt
1 tablespoon (15 ml) white wine vinegar
2 tomatoes
1 lime

1 2
3 4

| | | | | |
|---|---|---|---|---|
| 1 | Peel and finely slice the onions. Peel the garlic, remove and discard the germs and crush the cloves. Slice the chicken breasts into thin strips. | 2 | Heat the oil in a sauté pan or skillet over medium heat. Add the onions, cook for 5 minutes, then add the chicken breasts and garlic and lightly brown for 15 minutes. | |
| 3 | Add the turmeric and pepper and mix, and then add the tomato puree and bring to a boil. Reduce the heat, cover and cook for 15 minutes. | 4 | Peel the eggplants and cut them in half, then into quarters. | ➢ |

| | | | | | |
|---|---|---|---|---|---|
| 5 | Whisk the egg whites with ½ teaspoon (2 ml) salt and the vinegar until foamy. | 6 | Coat the eggplant quarters in the egg white mixutre and fry in ¼ inch (0.5 cm) oil. Let the cooked eggplant drain on paper towels. | 7 | Peel the tomatoes, cut them into quarters and seed them. |
| 8 | Place the cooked eggplant on the chicken, then add the tomatoes. Cover and cook for 30 minutes. | 9 | Juice the lime and mix the juice with 1 teaspoon (5 ml) salt. | 10 | Pour the seasoned lime juice between the eggplant quarters. Mix by tilting the pan. |

| 11 | Cook for 15 minutes, uncovered, and serve. | **"LIGHT" FRYING**<br>※<br>Coating the eggplant with the egg white mixture helps to prevent the eggplant from absorbing the cooking oil during the frying process. |
|---|---|---|
| | **SERVING SUGGESTION**<br>※<br>☞ Khoresh is traditionally served with chelo (Iranian rice, see recipe 31). | |

# TARATOR SAUCE

❧ **YIELD: ⁷⁄₈ CUP (200 ML)** • **PREPARATION: 10 MINUTES** ❧

1 garlic clove
3 lemons (for 7 tablespoons/105 ml juice)

½ teaspoon (2 ml) salt
¼ cup (60 ml) tahini

1 2
3 4

| | | | |
|---|---|---|---|
| 1 | Peel the garlic, remove and discard the germ and very finely chop the clove. | 2 | Juice the lemons. |
| 3 | Place the garlic, salt and lemon juice in a bowl. Mix. | 4 | Add the tahini and mix by gradually adding water until you obtain a smooth cream. Store, sealed, in the refrigerator. |

3

# COUSCOUS

❖ **YIELD: 4 SERVINGS** • PREPARATION: 20 MINUTES • COOKING: 10 TO 40 MINUTES ❖

2 cups (500 ml) poultry stock, preferably
   chicken (or 1 chicken bouillon cube)
2 cups (500 ml) fine traditional couscous
   (not instant)

2 tablespoons (30 ml) butter, cut into small
   pieces

**PRELIMINARY:**
Bring 1⅛ cups (300 ml) poultry stock to
a simmer in the lower part of a couscous-
maker or in a pressure cooker.

1 2
3 4

| | | | |
|---|---|---|---|
| 1 | Pour the couscous into a large, deep dish. Pour remaining ⅞ cup (200 ml) stock over top. | 2 | Mix using a spoon, then rub between your hands to help the stock penetrate. Let rest for 5 minutes, until the grains swell. |
| 3 | Distribute the couscous over the entire surface of the upper part of the couscous-maker. Leave covered until the steam escapes through the grains (about 5 to 35 minutes). | 4 | Return the couscous to the large dish and distribute the butter over the entire surface. ➤ |

| | | |
|---|---|---|
| **5** | Return the couscous to the upper part of the couscous-maker and leave until the steam passes through the couscous. | **TIP** ❋<br><br>☞ When using a couscous-maker, consider tying a dish towel around the upper and lower halves to prevent steam from escaping. If you don't have a couscous-maker or pressure cooker, cook the couscous according to this recipe but without steaming. To do this, increase the amount of stock incorporated into the couscous slightly (use 1¼ cups/300 ml for 2 cups/500 ml couscous). |

| | | | COOKING |
|---|---|---|---|
| 6 | Lower the heat of the stock and leave the couscous in the couscous-maker until you're ready to serve. | | The cooking time varies a lot depending on how strongly the stock is boiling. If cooking over a stew, the stock will be simmering and the couscous will take longer to cook (about 35 minutes). If cooking over stock only, the stock is more likely to be at a rolling boil and the couscous will cook quickly (5 to 10 minutes). |

# CHELO (IRANIAN RICE)

❖ **YIELD: 4 SERVINGS** • PREPARATION: 10 MINUTES • COOKING: 1 HOUR ❖

1½ cups (375 ml) basmati rice
½ cup (125 ml) plain yogurt
2⅔ cups (650 ml) water

2 teaspoons (10 ml) coarse salt
6 tablespoons (90 ml) butter, softened and
cut into pieces

| | | | | | |
|---|---|---|---|---|---|
| 1 | Pour plenty of water over the rice. Mix. Discard the water. Repeat twice to ensure the rice is well rinsed. Drain. | 2 | Thin the yogurt with a little water then add the 2⅔ cups (650 ml) water. | 3 | Place the drained rice in a saucepan. Add the yogurt, salt and butter. |
| 4 | Bring to a boil. Let simmer until the water is half absorbed and the escaping steam has poked holes in the rice. | 5 | Fluff, cover and cook for 45 minutes over medium heat. The rice is ready when its edges are golden. | 6 | Remove the lid and replace it with a flat plate. Turn the saucepan over and turn out the rice. Serve. |

# HERB CHELO

### VARIATION OF CHELO
❋

Start the chelo recipe (see recipe 31) and begin cooking the rice over high heat. Wash and dry ⅔ ounce (20 g) chives, ⅓ ounce (10 g) cilantro and ⅔ ounce (20 g) flat-leaf parsley. Chop off and discard the cilantro and parsley stems. Mince the chives and the cilantro and parsley leaves. Once the steam has poked holes in the rice (after step 4), add the herbs, fluff and continue cooking, covered. This rice goes well with fish dishes.

# DATE CHELO

## VARIATION OF CHELO

Pit 4½ ounces (125 g) dates and cut into quarters. Mince 1 onion. Zest ½ orange. Heat 2 tablespoons (30 ml) oil and lightly brown the onions for 5 minutes. Add the dates, zest and ½ teaspoon (2 ml) ground cinnamon. Cook for 2 minutes, stirring. Season with salt and pepper. Prepare the chelo (see recipe 31). Once the rice has holes from the steam, add the date mixture, mix and continue cooking.

# RICE PILAF

❧ **YIELD: 4 SERVINGS • PREPARATION: 15 MINUTES • COOKING: 20 MINUTES** ❧

1 onion
3 tablespoons (45 ml) butter
1½ cups (375 ml) long-grain rice
   (preferably basmati)

2⅔ cups (650 ml) water
1½ teaspoons (7 ml) coarse salt
Pepper, to taste

**PRELIMINARY:**
Cut out a circle of parchment paper the circumference of the inside of the saucepan in which you'll be cooking the rice.

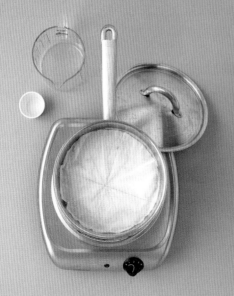

| 1 | Peel and mince the onion. | 2 | Melt the butter over medium heat. Add the onion and let soften, without browning. Add the rice and stir for 3 minutes. |
|---|---|---|---|
| 3 | Pour the water over the rice, bring to a boil, season with salt and then place the parchment paper circle on the water. Cover and cook over low heat for 12 to 15 minutes. | 4 | Take the saucepan off the heat, remove the parchment paper circle, season with pepper, fluff with a fork and serve. |

# PITA

❧ **YIELD: 6 PITAS** • **PREPARATION: 35 MINUTES** • **RESTING: 1 TO 2 HOURS** • **COOKING: 12 TO 24 MINUTES** ❧

1 teaspoon (5 ml) dry active yeast
½ cup + 1 tablespoon (140 ml) warm water
   (95°F to 105°F/35°C to 40°C)
2 cups (500 ml) all-purpose or bread flour

1 teaspoon (5 ml) salt
2 tablespoons + 1 teaspoon (35 ml) olive oil

**PRELIMINARY:**
Pour 1 tablespoon (15 ml) warm water over
the yeast. Wait 15 minutes. If using fresh
active yeast, mix with water using a fork,
but there's no need to wait 15 minutes.

| 1 | Mix the flour and salt in a large bowl. Set aside. | 2 | Mix the yeast granules and water until the mixture becomes foamy. | 3 | Pour ½ cup (125 ml) water over the yeast and mix. |
|---|---|---|---|---|---|
| 4 | Add this mixture to the flour and mix with a spatula. | 5 | Add 2 tablespoons (30 ml) oil as the mixture starts to come together and mix until a dough forms. | 6 | Knead the dough until it no longer sticks to your fingers. Form a ball. ➤ |

7  8
9 10

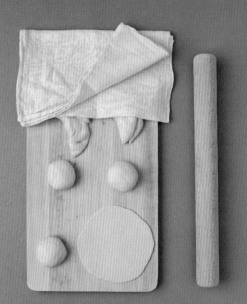

| 7 | Pour 1 teaspoon (5 ml) oil into a bowl and roll the dough around until it's covered with oil (to keep it from drying out). Cover with plastic wrap. | 8 | Let the dough rise in a warm place for 45 minutes to 2 hours, until it doubles in volume. |
|---|---|---|---|
| 9 | Preheat the oven to its maximum temperature (minimum 500°F/250°C) and place a baking sheet on the middle rack. Gently punch down the dough ball to remove any air. | 10 | Cut the dough ball into 6 pieces and form balls. To form the balls, fold the dough over itself from underneath. Arrange the balls on a dish towel. On a floured surface, roll out each ball to about ⅛ inch (3 mm) thick. |

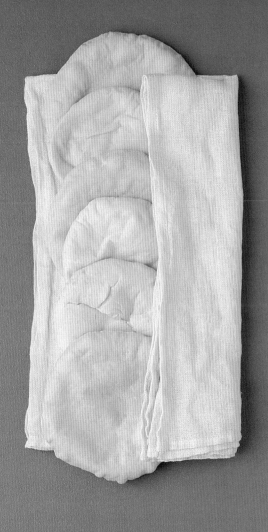

| 11 | Once the oven reaches its highest temperature, slide a dough circle onto the baking sheet. It should rise (like a balloon) and brown very lightly (2 to 4 minutes). Remove the pita and immediately wrap it in a dish towel so it remains soft. Wait until the oven returns to maximum temperature and continue baking the dough circles. | **TIPS** ❈ <br><br> ☛ Use a rolling pin to roll out the dough. <br><br> ☛ Lightly flour the dough circles before placing them in the oven so they don't stick to the baking sheet. |
|---|---|---|

# CHEESE LAVASH

❧ **YIELD: 6 PIECES** • PREPARATION: 30 MINUTES • RESTING: 20 MINUTES • COOKING: 36 MINUTES ❧

2½ cups (625 ml) bread flour
1 teaspoon (5 ml) salt
1 tablespoon (15 ml) oil

½ cup (125 ml) plain yogurt
7 tablespoons (105 ml) water, room
    temperature

4 ounces (120 g) soft cheese (such as
    Laughing Cow)

1 2
3 4

| 1 | Mix the flour, salt, oil and yogurt in a large bowl using a spatula. | 2 | Add the water and mix with the spatula. | |
|---|---|---|---|---|
| 3 | Once a dough forms, place on a work surface (not floured) and knead until well-mixed, about 1 minute. Continue kneading until the dough is no longer sticky. Form a ball. Cover and let rest for 20 minutes. | 4 | Mix the cheese with a little water, if necessary, to obtain a cream that spreads easily. | ➢ |

5 6
7 8

| 5 | Divide the dough into 6 pieces and shape into balls by folding the dough over itself from underneath. | 6 | On a floured work surface and using a floured rolling pin, roll out the first piece of dough into a very thin pancake. |
|---|---|---|---|
| 7 | Spread the cheese mixture over the upper half of the pancake, leaving a ½-inch (1 cm) border. Fold the lower half over the upper half and seal by pressing the edges firmly together. | 8 | Heat a non-stick skillet over high heat. Place the first dough half-circle in the skillet, lower the heat to medium-high and cook for 3 minutes. Turn the lavash over and cook for another 3 minutes. |

| 9 | Take the lavash out of the skillet and place in a dish towel. Start again with the other dough half-circles, watching the heat: the skillet needs to be hot enough to lightly brown the lavash, but not so hot that the lavash burns when cooked 3 minutes per side. |
|---|---|

**VARIATION**
❈

You can substitute a stronger-tasting cheese, such as feta, for the soft cheese.

**TIP**
❈

☛ Lavash reheats well. Place it in a warm oven (210°F to 265°F/100°C to 130°C) for 5 minutes.

# 4

## COUSCOUS & TAGINES

## PAN-FRIED MEATS

## OVEN-ROASTED MEATS

# SEVEN-VEGETABLE COUSCOUS

**❖ YIELD: 4 SERVINGS • PREPARATION: 35 MINUTES • COOKING: 1 HOUR ❖**

2 cups (500 ml) poultry stock (or 1 chicken bouillon cube)
1½-pounds (600 g) lamb shoulder, boned and cut into 12 pieces
2 carrots
2 tomatoes
3 turnips
1 zucchini

1 green bell pepper
1 red onion
⅓ ounce (10 g) fresh ginger
½ mild fresh chili pepper
1 teaspoon (5 ml) coriander seeds
2 tablespoons (30 ml) olive oil
2 pinches saffron
½ teaspoon (2 ml) ground allspice

9 ounces (250 g) chickpeas, cooked, drained & rinsed
**FOR THE COUSCOUS:**
1 cup (250 ml) poultry stock (or 1 chicken bouillon cube)
2 cups (500 ml) fine couscous
2 tablespoons (30 ml) butter
**PRELIMINARY:** Bring all of the poultry stock to a simmer. Take the meat out of the refrigerator.

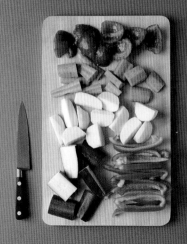

1 2
3 4

| | | | |
|---|---|---|---|
| 1 | Peel the carrots, tomatoes and turnips. Cut the carrots and zucchini in half lengthwise and then into thirds. Cut the turnips and tomatoes into quarters and seed the tomatoes. Seed the bell pepper and slice it into strips. | 2 | Peel the onion and cut it into quarters. Peel and grate the ginger. |
| 3 | Wash the chili pepper and crush it along with the coriander seeds with a mortar and pestle until you obtain a pasty mixture. | 4 | Heat the oil over high heat. Brown the meat (in several portions, if needed). Transfer the meat to a plate and lower the heat under the pot a little.    ➤ |

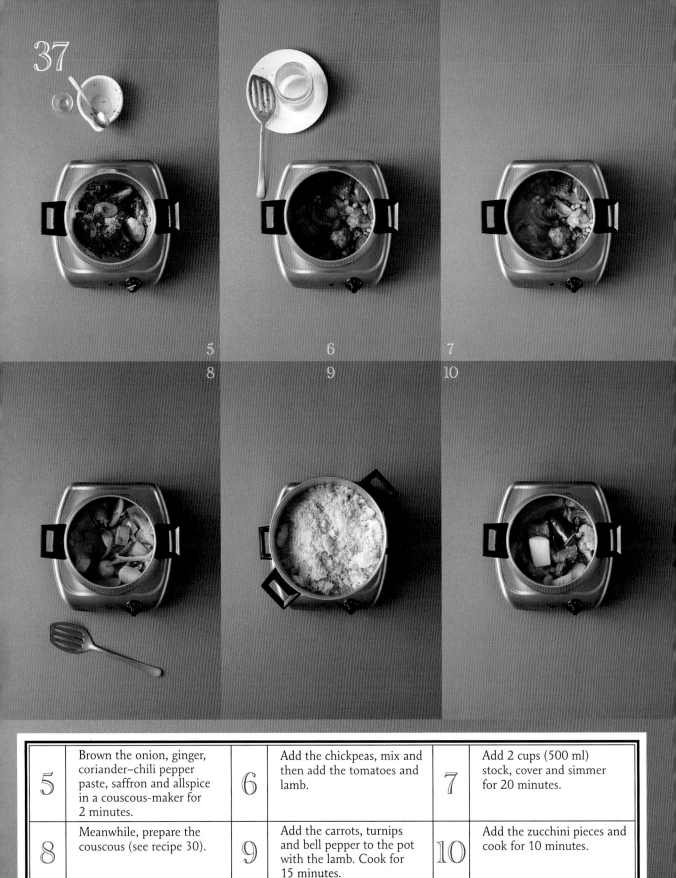

| 5 | Brown the onion, ginger, coriander–chili pepper paste, saffron and allspice in a couscous-maker for 2 minutes. | 6 | Add the chickpeas, mix and then add the tomatoes and lamb. | 7 | Add 2 cups (500 ml) stock, cover and simmer for 20 minutes. |
|---|---|---|---|---|---|
| 8 | Meanwhile, prepare the couscous (see recipe 30). | 9 | Add the carrots, turnips and bell pepper to the pot with the lamb. Cook for 15 minutes. | 10 | Add the zucchini pieces and cook for 10 minutes. |

| 11 | Serve the couscous and stew in a deep dish. |
|---|---|

### VARIATION
❊

If tomatoes are not in season, we strongly recommend you substitute 1½ teaspoons (7 ml) tomato paste for the fresh tomatoes.

### COOKING CHICKPEAS
❊

To cook dried chickpeas, soak them in a large quantity of water for 12 hours with ½ teaspoon (2 ml) baking soda. Drain and cook in enough water to completely cover the chickpeas. Cook over low heat, covered, for 30 minutes to 1 hour. Add the chickpeas and their cooking water to the meat preparation at step 6.

# CHICKEN COUSCOUS

➤ **YIELD: 4 SERVINGS** • PREPARATION: 40 MINUTES • COOKING: 1 HOUR ➤

4 large chicken legs
1 teaspoon (5 ml) ground ginger
1 pinch saffron
⅓ cup (75 ml) olive oil
1 pound (500 g) onions
2 cups (500 ml) poultry stock (or 1 chicken
  bouillon cube)

3½ ounces (100 g) raisins
  (about ⅔ cup/150 ml)
1½ tablespoons (22 ml) sugar
½ mild fresh chili pepper
1 tomato
2 garlic cloves

**FOR THE COUSCOUS:**
2 cups (500 ml) fine couscous
2 tablespoons (30 ml) butter
1 cup (250 ml) poultry stock (or 1 chicken
  bouillon cube)

1 2
3 4

| 1 | Cut the chicken legs in half. Score the skin 2 to 4 times with a knife. | 2 | Mix the ginger, saffron and 2 tablespoons (30 ml) oil. | |
|---|---|---|---|---|
| 3 | Coat the meat in the oil and spice mixture, cover and let rest at room temperature while you prepare the rest of the recipe. | 4 | Put 1 onion aside. Peel the other onions, cut them in half and slice them. Bring all of the stock to a simmer. Soak the raisins in a little water. | ➢ |

5 6
7 8

| 5 | Heat 2 tablespoons (30 ml) oil in a large skillet over medium-high heat and brown the onions. Sprinkle the sugar overtop and mix. | 6 | Add about 7 tablespoons (105 ml) stock, to cover the onions. Cook, barely simmering, for 15 minutes, uncovered. |
|---|---|---|---|
| 7 | Drain the raisins, add to the onions and cook for another 10 minutes, until the stock evaporates. Take the pan off the heat. | 8 | Wash the chili pepper and crush with a mortar and pestle. Peel the tomato, cut it into quarters and seed it. Peel and mince the remaining onion. Peel the garlic, remove and discard the germs and finely chop the cloves. |

| 9 | Heat the bottom part of a couscous-maker over high heat with 1 tablespoon (15 ml) olive oil and brown the chicken legs on all sides, beginning with the skin side. | **TIP**<br>❇<br>To avoid lowering the temperature of the oil, it's better to cook the chicken legs in several batches. | ➤ |

10 11
12 13

| 10 | Lower the heat to medium and add the tomato, onion, garlic and chili pepper to the chicken legs. | 11 | Mix and add enough stock to half-fill the couscous-maker (about 1⅔ cups/400 ml). Simmer for 25 minutes. |
|----|---|----|---|
| 12 | Meanwhile, prepare the couscous (see recipe 30). | 13 | Reheat the onion and caramelized raisin garnish over medium heat. |

| 14 | Serve the stew and couscous with the caramelized raisins and onion on the side. |
|---|---|

# LAMB & APRICOT TAGINE

➤ **YIELD: 4 SERVINGS** • PREPARATION: 15 MINUTES • COOKING: 50 MINUTES ◄

- 4½ tablespoons (67 ml) butter
- 2 tablespoons (30 ml) neutral oil (such as grapeseed, canola or sunflower)
- 1¾- pounds leg of lamb, cut into 15 to 20 pieces

- ½ teaspoon (2 ml) salt
- ¼ teaspoon (1 ml) pepper
- ¼ teaspoon (1 ml) ground ginger
- 1½ cups (375 ml) water
- 1 cinnamon stick

- 9 ounces (250 g) dried apricots
- ¼ cup (60 ml) sugar
- ½ teaspoon (2 ml) ground cinnamon
- 1¾ ounces (50 g) sliced almonds (about 7 tablespoons/105 ml)

1 2
3 4

| | | | |
|---|---|---|---|
| 1 | Melt 3 tablespoons (45 ml) butter and 1 table-spoon (15 ml) oil in a sauté pan or skillet over medium-high heat. Brown the lamb. | 2 | Add the salt, pepper and ginger and mix. |
| 3 | Half-fill the pan with water (about 1 cup/ 250 ml), add the cinnamon stick and bring to a boil. Pour into a tagine (loosening any bits stuck to the bottom of the pan). Cover and cook for ½ hour over low heat. | 4 | Wash the apricots. Cut into quarters. ➤ |

5 6
7 8

| 5 | Mix ½ cup (125 ml) water along with the sugar, ground cinnamon, 1½ tablespoons (22 ml) butter and the apricots in a small saucepan. Bring to a boil. | 6 | Cook over low heat until the sauce thickens a little, about 5 minutes. |
|---|---|---|---|
| 7 | Heat 1 tablespoon (15 ml) oil in a skillet and toast the almonds, stirring regularly. | 8 | Transfer the almonds to paper towels. |

9   Take the lamb out of its cooking liquid and discard the liquid. Cover the lamb with the apricot sauce and sprinkle the almonds on top. Serve.

### TIP
❊

If you don't have a tagine, you can cook the entire dish in a sauté pan or large skillet.

### SERVING SUGGESTION
❊

 The caramelized apricot sauce can be used on a dessert, such as vanilla ice cream.

# LAMB & PRUNE TAGINE

❧ YIELD: 4 SERVINGS • PREPARATION: 20 MINUTES • MARINATING: 2 HOURS • COOKING: 1 HOUR, 45 MINUTES ❧

2 cups (500 ml) poultry stock (or 1 chicken
  bouillon cube)
2 onions
2 garlic cloves
¼ cup (60 ml) olive oil
1 teaspoon (5 ml) ground ginger

1 teaspoon (5 ml) ground cinnamon
1 pinch saffron
Salt & pepper, to taste
4½- pounds (2 kg) lamb shoulder, boned
  and cut into 12 pieces
20 pitted prunes

2½ ounces (70 g) blanched almonds (about
  ½ cup/125 ml)
1 tablespoon (15 ml) sesame seeds
**PRELIMINARY:**
Bring the stock to a simmer.

| 1 | Peel the onions, cut them in half and then finely chop them. Peel the garlic, remove and discard the germs and crush the cloves. | 2 | Make a marinade by mixing 3 tablespoons (45 ml) oil with the ginger, cinnamon, saffron, garlic and onions in a bowl. Season with salt and pepper. | |
|---|---|---|---|---|
| 3 | Coat the pieces of lamb in the marinade, cover and allow to marinate for 2 hours at room temperature. | 4 | Heat the remaining oil in a large sauté pan or skillet over medium-high heat and brown the meat. | ➤ |

5 6
7 8

| 5 | Add enough simmering stock to half-fill the pan. Transfer the meat to a tagine, cover and cook over low heat for 1 hour and 15 minutes. | 6 | Add the prunes and continue cooking for 15 minutes, uncovered, over medium heat. |
|---|---|---|---|
| 7 | Toast the almonds in a dry skillet (without fat) over medium heat. | 8 | Toast the sesame seeds using the same method. |

9 Sprinkle the almonds and the sesame seeds over the tagine, then serve.

### WITHOUT A TAGINE
❋

If you don't intend to serve the dish in a tagine (or you don't have a tagine), you can instead cook everything in a sauté pan or large skillet. (A sauté pan is similar to a skillet and has wide, flared sides.)

### TIP
❋

Before transferring the contents of the sauté pan to the tagine, take care to loosen any bits of meat stuck the bottom of the pan using a wooden spoon or heatproof spatula. This is concentrated, caramelized flavor!

# CHICKEN & ALMOND TAGINE

➤ YIELD: 4 SERVINGS • PREPARATION: 30 MINUTES • COOKING: 1½ HOURS ➤

2 tablespoons (30 ml) olive oil
2 pinches saffron
4 red onions
1 garlic clove
½ ounce (15 g) fresh ginger

½ lemon
2¼ pounds (1 kg) chicken legs
1 tablespoon (15 ml) butter
1¼ cups (310 ml) poultry stock, preferably
  chicken (or ½ chicken bouillon cube)

Pepper, to taste
5 ounces (150 g) blanched almonds
  (about 1 cup/250 ml)
**PRELIMINARY:**
Mix 1 tablespoon (15 ml) oil with the saffron.

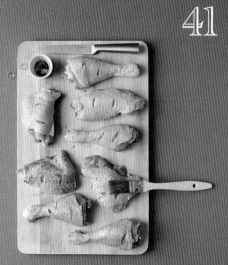

1 2
3 4

| 1 | Peel and mince the onions. Peel and finely chop the garlic. Peel and grate the ginger. Juice the lemon. | 2 | Cut the chicken legs in half at the joint. Score the skin. Coat with the saffron oil. | |
|---|---|---|---|---|
| 3 | Melt the butter and remaining oil in a large sauté pan or skillet over medium-high heat. Brown the chicken on all sides. Take the chicken pieces out of the pan and set aside. | 4 | Cook the onions and garlic in the same pan over medium heat. Mix well. When they start to brown, cover and cook for 20 minutes. | ➤ |

5  6
7  8

| 5 | Add the stock to the onions and garlic and bring to a boil, scraping the bottom of the pan with a spatula to loosen any small bits stuck there. | 6 | Place the pieces of chicken in a tagine, then pour the contents of the sauté pan overtop. |
|---|---|---|---|
| 7 | Add the ginger. Season with pepper and mix. | 8 | Cover and cook for 45 minutes over low heat. |

| 9 | Uncover and allow the sauce to thicken for 15 minutes. Add the lemon juice and almonds and mix. Cover and serve hot. | **TIP**<br>❋<br>You can enhance the flavor of the almonds by toasting them for a few minutes. Heat the almonds in a dry medium-sized skillet (without any fat). Stir regularly to ensure they brown but do not burn. |

# PAN-FRIED LAMB CHOPS

➤ **YIELD: 4 SERVINGS** • PREPARATION: 5 MINUTES • COOKING: 7 MINUTES ➤

| | | |
|---|---|---|
| 1 teaspoon (5 ml) ground cinnamon | 1 teaspoon (5 ml) ground coriander | 8 lamb rib chops |
| 1 teaspoon (5 ml) ground cumin | 1½ tablespoons (22 ml) butter | 2 tablespoons (30 ml) rose water |
| 1 teaspoon (5 ml) ground nutmeg | 1 tablespoon (15 ml) oil | ½ teaspoon (2 ml) salt |

1 2
3 4

| | | | |
|---|---|---|---|
| 1 | Mix the cinnamon, cumin, nutmeg and coriander. | 2 | Heat the butter and oil in a skillet over medium-high heat. Fry the chops for 3 minutes on each side. |
| 3 | Take the chops out of the skillet. Off the heat, pour the spice mixture into the skillet. Mix. | 4 | Deglaze the skillet with the rose water and mix. Return the skillet to medium heat. Reheat both sides of the chops in the seasoned sauce for 30 seconds. Season with salt and serve. |

# CHICKEN WITH OLIVES & LEMONS

**➤ YIELD: 4 SERVINGS • PREPARATION: 35 MINUTES • COOKING: 1½ HOURS ➤**

1 onion
3 garlic cloves
1 teaspoon (5 ml) salt
1 teaspoon (5 ml) pepper
4 chicken legs
2½ tablespoons (37 ml) butter

2 tablespoons (30 ml) olive oil
1 teaspoon (5 ml) ground ginger
1 teaspoon (5 ml) ras el hanout
2 cups (500 ml) water
⅓ ounce (10 g) cilantro
⅔ ounce (20 g) flat-leaf parsley

3¾ ounces (110 g) green or black olives, pitted
2 preserved lemons
**PRELIMINARY:** Peel and mince the onion. Peel the garlic, slice in half, remove and discard the germs and crush the cloves.

1 2
3 4

| 1 | Mix half the salt and pepper and sprinkle over the chicken legs (top and bottom). | 2 | Melt the butter with the olive oil in a sauté pan or skillet over high heat. Brown the chicken, skin side first. Take the browned chicken out of the pan and lower the heat. | |
|---|---|---|---|---|
| 3 | Place the onion in the pan and let soften, stirring often. Add the garlic and mix. Add the ginger, ras el hanout and the remaining pepper and salt and mix. | 4 | Add the water, mix, return the chicken legs to the pan and bring to a boil. Cover and simmer over medium-low heat for 1 hour. | ➤ |

5 6
7 8

| 5 | Wash and dry the cilantro and parsley and pluck the leaves from the stems. Gather the leaves, roll them up tightly and mince. Rinse and drain the olives. | 6 | Cut the preserved lemons into quarters, remove and discard the flesh and rinse the skin well. Dry and cut each quarter into slivers. |
|---|---|---|---|
| 7 | Add the preserved lemon pieces, olives, parsley and cilantro to the pan. Mix and cook for another 15 minutes, covered. | 8 | Uncover and take the chicken legs out of the pan. Raise the heat to high and reduce the sauce for 5 to 7 minutes, until it thickens a little. |

| 9 | Place the chicken legs in a serving dish and sprinkle a little sauce on top. Pour the extra sauce into a small bowl and serve on the side. | **TIP** ✹ <br> ☞ If the dish can't be served immediately, it's not a problem. This is the big advantage of this type of dish (including tagines): they improve while simmering. In the case of this dish, return the chicken legs to the pan, coat well with sauce, cover and simmer over very low heat while waiting to serve. |

# KOFTAS (MEATBALLS) & EGGS

**❖ YIELD: 4 SERVINGS • PREPARATION: 30 MINUTES • COOKING: 8 MINUTES ❖**

⅓ ounce (10 g) cilantro
⅔ ounce (20 g) parsley
1 onion
1 pound (500 g) ground beef
1 teaspoon (5 ml) ground cumin

2 teaspoons (10 ml) paprika
3 pinches cayenne pepper
1 teaspoon (5 ml) + 1 pinch salt
1 to 2 tablespoons (15 to 30 ml) water

1 to 3 tablespoons oil (15 to 45 ml) + 2 or 3
  tablespoons (30 to 45 ml) for your hands
3 tablespoons (45 ml) butter
8 eggs
Pepper, to taste

1 2
3 4

| 1 | Wash and dry the cilantro and parsley and pluck the leaves from the stems. Gather the leaves and roll them up tightly. Mince. | 2 | Peel and very finely mince the onion. | |
|---|---|---|---|---|
| 3 | Put the beef, onion, cilantro, parsley, cumin, paprika, cayenne pepper and 1 teaspoon (5 ml) salt in a large bowl. Mix using your hands, adding oil and water to obtain a supple texture. | 4 | Pour a little oil into a container and oil your hands. Form small meatballs, the koftas, by rolling the meat mixture in the palms of your hands. | ➤ |

| 5 | Melt the butter in a large skillet over high heat and brown the koftas. | **TIP**<br><br>If the koftas release a lot of juice, take them out of the pan with a skimmer and reduce the juice over high heat before returning the koftas to the pan and lowering the heat to medium-high. |

| | | | TIP |
|---|---|---|---|
| 6 | Carefully break the eggs between the koftas and fry the eggs until the whites are firm (the yolks should remain runny). Sprinkle a little black pepper and salt overtop and serve. | | ☞ The kofta mixture has a good texture when it's supple and doesn't fall apart while mixing. Add as much oil and water as needed to achieve this. |

# ROSEMARY, GARLIC & LEMON CHICKEN

**❖ YIELD: 4 TO 6 SERVINGS • PREPARATION: 20 MINUTES • COOKING: 2½ TO 3 HOURS ❖**

1 garlic head
1 lemon
1 tablespoon (15 ml) olive oil
½ teaspoon (2 ml) turmeric

1 (3½- to 4½-pound/1.5 to 2 kg) chicken
Salt & pepper, to taste
2 sprigs rosemary

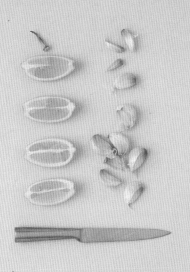

| 1 | Separate the cloves of the garlic head without peeling them. Cut the lemon into quarters. | 2 | Mix the oil and turmeric. Brush the chicken with this mixture. Season with salt and pepper. |
|---|---|---|---|
| 3 | Place the chicken in the center of a casserole dish or Dutch oven and arrange the garlic cloves, rosemary sprigs and lemon quarters around it. | 4 | Cover and place in a cold oven. Heat the oven to 300°F (150°C) and cook for 2½ hours if the chicken weighs 3½ pounds (1.5 kg) or 3 hours if it weighs 4½ pounds (2 kg). ➤ |

| | Strain the pan juices to make a sauce. | **TIP** ✳ |
|---|---|---|
| 5 | | Since turmeric colors the skin, use vinyl or latex gloves to avoid having yellow fingers! |

| 6 | Cut the chicken into pieces and serve with the sauce, roasted garlic cloves, lemon quarters and rosemary sprigs. | **VARIATION**<br>✻<br>You can also peel the roasted garlic cloves and mix the flesh into the sauce so the sauce has more texture and flavor. |
|---|---|---|

# ROASTED LAMB

❧ **YIELD: 4 SERVINGS** • **PREPARATION: 25 MINUTES** • **MARINATING: 1 HOUR** • **COOKING: 2½ HOURS** ❧

3½-pound (1.6 kg) lamb shoulder, boned,
  leaving 1¾ to 2¼ pounds (0.8 to 1 kg)
  meat, rolled and tied
½ teaspoon (2 ml) ras el hanout
Salt & pepper, to taste
⅓ cup (75 ml) olive oil

⅓ cup (75 ml) raisins
1 ounce (30 g) fresh ginger
1 onion
1 garlic clove
1½ tablespoons (22 ml) honey
2 pinches saffron

1¼ cups (310 ml) poultry stock, preferably
  chicken (or ½ chicken bouillon cube)
1¾ ounces (50 g) blanched almonds (about
  ⅓ cup/75 ml)

1 2
3 4

| | | | |
|---|---|---|---|
| 1 | Place the meat in a dish. Sprinkle ras el hanout and salt overtop and coat with olive oil, saving 1 tablespoon (15 ml). Cover with plastic wrap and marinate for 1 hour in the refrigerator. | 2 | Preheat the oven to 300°F (150°C). Place the raisins in a little warm water and leave to soak. Peel and grate the ginger. |
| 3 | Peel the onion, cut it in half and mince it. Peel the garlic, remove and discard the germ and finely chop the clove. Drain the raisins. | 4 | Heat the spoonful of oil over high heat in an ovenproof pot. Brown the shoulder on all sides. Take the shoulder out of the pot and lower the heat to medium. ➤ |

5 6
7 8

| 5 | Place the onions in the pot and brown for a few minutes. Add the ginger, the oil from the marinade dish and the honey. Mix. | 6 | Put the lamb shoulder back in the pot and add the saffron, garlic and raisins. |
|---|---|---|---|
| 7 | Add 1 cup (250 ml) of stock and bake for 2 hours and 15 minutes. Watch the level of stock in the pot: if too much evaporates, add the remaining stock. The stock should be reduced and shiny once the lamb has finished cooking. | 8 | Shortly before the lamb finishes cooking, toast the almonds in a dry skillet over medium-high heat. Coarsely chop the toasted nuts. |

| 9 | Just before serving, remove the twine from around the meat by cutting it with a pair of scissors. Sprinkle the almonds overtop, add a little freshly ground pepper and cover the shoulder with its juice. | **SERVING SUGGESTION** |
|---|---|---|
| | | Serve with couscous (see recipe 30). |

# OVEN-BAKED KIBBEH

⇻ YIELD: 25 TO 30 KIBBEH • PREPARATION: 50 MINUTES • COOKING: 1 HOUR ⇺

25 ounces (700 g) leg of lamb
12½ ounces (350 g) fine bulgur
(about 2 cups/500 ml)
6 onions

⅔ cup (150 ml) olive oil
⅔ cup (150 ml) pine nuts
2 teaspoons (10 ml) salt + more, to taste
Pepper, to taste

**PRELIMINARY:**
Finely dice the meat and set it aside in the refrigerator. Soak the bulgur in plenty of cold water for 10 minutes. Preheat the oven to 350°F (180°C).

| | | | | | |
|---|---|---|---|---|---|
| 1 | Peel and chop onions. Blend the meat in a food processor. Set 1 pound (500 g) aside in the refrigerator. | 2 | Heat 7 tablespoons (105 ml) olive oil in a sauté pan or skillet over medium heat and brown the pine nuts. | 3 | Take the pine nuts out of the pan with a skimmer, leaving the oil behind. Add the onions and brown for 10 minutes. |
| 4 | Squeeze the bulgur between your hands to remove as much liquid as possible. Set the bulgur aside. | 5 | Add the room temperature ground meat to the onions. Season with salt and pepper, and cook for 10 minutes. | 6 | Set aside a large spoonful of pine nuts. Add the rest of the pine nuts to the skillet, off the heat. ➤ |

7 8
9 10

| 7 | Mix the refrigerated meat, bulgur and 2 tea-spoons (10 ml) salt. Blend in a food processor until you obtain a very creamy paste. | 8 | Grease a large cooking dish with 1 tablespoon (15 ml) oil. |
|---|---|---|---|
| 9 | Press half of the meat paste against the bottom of the dish. Distribute the meat, onion and pine nut filling on top. | 10 | Between moistened palms, form thin pancakes with the remaining paste. Place on top of the filling. Seal by pressing with your moistened fingers. Cut out diamond-shaped kibbehs. |

| 11 | Lightly press a pine nut into the center of each diamond, and then brush everything with the rest of the oil. Bake for about 40 to 45 minutes, until the surface is firm and brown. | **TIP**<br>❋<br>For a successful filling, break up the ground meat as it cooks to keep it from sticking together and forming clumps. Stop cooking once the water released by the meat has evaporated. |

# MOUSSAKA

❧ YIELD: 6 TO 8 SERVINGS • PREPARATION: 1 HOUR • COOKING: 1 HOUR, 10 MINUTES ❧

2¼ pounds (1 kg) eggplant
Salt & pepper, to taste
⅓ ounce (10 g) parsley
1 onion
2 eggs
¼ cup (60 ml) butter

1⅔ pounds (750 g) ground beef
1 tablespoon (15 ml) tomato paste
¼ cup (60 ml) red wine
¼ cup (60 ml) water
1½ ounces (40 g) white sandwich bread
    (2 or 3 slices)

¼ cup (60 ml) flour
2 cups (500 ml) milk
Oil, to coat the eggplants
½ teaspoon (2 ml) ground cinnamon
¼ cup (60 ml) grated Parmesan

1 2
3 4

| | | | | |
|---|---|---|---|---|
| 1 | Rinse the eggplants, cut away the green end and peel every skin in strips. Slice lengthwise. | 2 | Place the eggplants in a strainer, sprinkle salt overtop and then place a weight on top. Let the eggplants release their water while preparing the rest of the recipe. | |
| 3 | Wash and dry the parsley and pluck the leaves from the stems. Gather the leaves, roll them up tightly and mince them. Peel and finely chop the onion. | 4 | Whisk the eggs lightly. | ➤ |

5 6
7 8

| | | | |
|---|---|---|---|
| 5 | Melt half the butter in a large skillet over medium-high heat. Add the onions and let soften and lightly brown (about 5 to 10 minutes). | 6 | Add the ground meat to the onions, season with salt and pepper and stir regularly until the meat browns. |
| 7 | Add the tomato paste, parsley, wine and water to the onion-meat mixture. Mix and let simmer until the liquid is absorbed. Set aside and let cool. | 8 | Remove the crusts from the bread. Process the bread in a food processor to make bread crumbs. |

9 10
11 12

| 9 | Melt the remaining butter over medium-low heat. Add the flour and mix to obtain a smooth mixture. Cook until foamy, stirring constantly. | 10 | Take the pan off the heat, add half the milk and whisk. Add the rest of the milk and whisk until the mixture is smooth and has no lumps. Season with salt and pepper. |
|---|---|---|---|
| 11 | Return the pan to the heat and bring to a boil. Simmer for 5 minutes, whisking constantly, until the sauce is creamy. | 12 | Pour a little sauce over the eggs, whisk and add to the sauce. Whisk for 2 minutes. Remove the sauce from the heat and cover. ➤ |

13 14
15 16

| 13 | Turn the oven's broiler on. Rinse and dry the eggplants. Arrange them on a baking sheet lined with aluminum foil and brush them with oil. Grill for 5 to 7 minutes. | 14 | Preheat the oven to 400°F (200°C) and move a rack to the middle of the oven. Add the cinnamon, half the bread crumbs and half the Parmesan to the meat mixture. |
|---|---|---|---|
| 15 | Sprinkle the rest of the bread crumbs into a baking dish. Arrange 1 or 2 layers of eggplant over the bread crumbs and top with half the meat mixture and a little sauce. | 16 | Arrange another layer or two of eggplant over the sauce and top with the rest of the meat mixture. |

**17** Pour the remaining sauce over the meat. Sprinkle the rest of the Parmesan on top and bake for 40 to 45 minutes, until the moussaka browns. Let cool for 5 to 10 minutes before cutting into slices.

**EXPRESS TIP**
❋

☛ If you are in a hurry, you can leave out step 2, during which the eggplants are left to drain. In this case, lightly season the eggplants with salt before grilling.

# CHICKEN BASTILLA

❧ **YIELD: 6 TO 8 SERVINGS • PREPARATION: 55 MINUTES • COOKING: 40 TO 45 MINUTES** ❧

14 ounces (400 g) onions
⅓ ounce (10 g) cilantro
⅔ ounce (20 g) parsley
4 ounces (120 g) blanched almonds (about
    ¾ cup/175 ml)
⅓ cup (75 ml) butter
1 tablespoon (15 ml) olive oil

4 boneless skinless chicken breasts
Salt, to taste
2 teaspoons (10 ml) ground cinnamon
1 teaspoon (5 ml) ras el hanout
2 tablespoons (30 ml) orange blossom water
7 tablespoons (105 ml) water
3 tablespoons (45 ml) granulated sugar

2 eggs
6 sheets brik or phyllo pastry
1 tablespoon (15 ml) confectioners' sugar
**PRELIMINARY:** Peel and mince the onions.
Wash and dry the cilantro and parsley, and
pluck the leaves from the stems. Gather the
leaves, roll them up tightly and mince.

1 2
3 4

| 1 | Toast the almonds in a small dry skillet (without any fat) over medium-high heat. | 2 | Melt 2 tablespoons (30 ml) butter and the oil in a large skillet over high heat. Season the chicken breasts with salt and brown well. Take the chicken out of the pan and lower the heat a little. | |
|---|---|---|---|---|
| 3 | In the same large skillet, brown the onions with a pinch of salt. Add the cinnamon and ras el hanout and mix. Add the orange blossom water, mix, then add the water and bring to a boil. | 4 | Return the chicken breasts to the skillet and cook for 10 minutes over low heat (turn the meat over halfway through). | ➤ |

| 5 | Prepare a caramel by browning the granulated sugar in a non-stick skillet. | 6 | Add the almonds and coat well. Take the coated almonds out of the skillet and let cool. | 7 | Take the chicken out the skillet and leave the liquid to reduce. Transfer the reduced liquid and onions to a bowl. |
|---|---|---|---|---|---|
| 8 | Divide the chicken into pieces using your fingers. Set aside 10 almonds and coarsely chop the rest. | 9 | Beat the eggs and add to the cooked onion mixture. Add the herbs and mix. Heat the oven to 400°F (200°C). | 10 | Melt the rest of the butter. Stack the pastry sheets and brush melted butter onto the first sheet. |

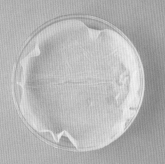

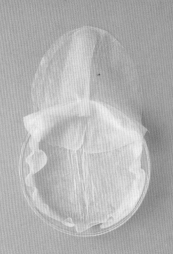

11 12
13 14

| 11 | Place the buttered pastry sheet in the center of a deep cake pan or round baking dish. Repeat with a second buttered pastry sheet. | 12 | Place a third buttered pastry sheet straddling the pan and the work surface, with half the sheet outside the pan. | |
|---|---|---|---|---|
| 13 | Repeat step 12 with 3 more pastry sheets, arranging them in a rosette pattern around the pan. | 14 | Pour half of the onion mixture into the center of the pastry-lined pan and level with the back of a spoon. | ➤ |

15 16
17 18

| 15 | Sprinkle half the almond pieces on top. | 16 | Distribute the chicken strips on top, then pour the remaining onions over the chicken. |
|----|------------------------------------------|----|----------------------------------------------------------------------------------------|
| 17 | Fold over the pastry sheets to seal the bastilla. Tuck any edges that stick out into the pan, around the edge of the bastilla. Sprinkle water overtop and bake for 10 to 15 minutes, until cripsy. | 18 | Turn the oven's broiler on. Using a strainer, sprinkle confectioners' sugar over the entire surface of the bastilla and caramelize under the broiler for a few seconds. |

| | |
|---|---|
| **19** | Garnish with whole almonds, then serve. |

**TIP**
❀

☛ It's important to lightly sprinkle the bastilla with water before baking so the brik pastry doesn't curl during cooking. Moisten your fingers and throw drops of water on the bastilla.

# SHISH KEBAB

❖ **YIELD: 4 SERVINGS** • PREPARATION: 40 MINUTES • MARINATING: 24 HOURS • COOKING: 6 TO 8 MINUTES ❖

1 sprig mint (about 8 leaves)
1 sprig rosemary
3 garlic cloves
1 lemon
3 tablespoons (45 ml) olive oil

1 teaspoon (5 ml) salt
Pepper, to taste
2¼- pounds (1 kg) leg of lamb (boned and trimmed)
1 yellow bell pepper

1 red bell pepper
1 orange bell pepper
1 red onion

| 1 | Wash and dry the mint and rosemary. Pluck the mint leaves from the stems. For the rosemary, slide two fingers backwards along the stem to remove the leaves. | 2 | Peel the garlic and remove the germ. Zest and juice ½ lemon. | |
|---|---|---|---|---|
| 3 | Place the mint, rosemary, zest, lemon juice, olive oil, salt, pepper and garlic in the bowl of a food processor. Blend for 1 minute; the marinade should remain fairly uniform. | 4 | Coarsely dice the meat. | ➤ |

5 6
7 8

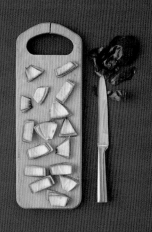

| 5 | Mix the meat and marinade in a freezer bag or in a sealed container. Set aside in the refrigerator for 24 hours. | 6 | Rinse the bell peppers. Cut off the ends, then split the peppers open. Remove the seeds and white membrane. Dice each pepper into about 20 squares. |
|---|---|---|---|
| 7 | Peel the red onion and cut it into quarters. Take the 3 outer layers of the onion, the thickest layers, and cut them into quarters. | 8 | Turn the oven's broiler on. Thread alternating pieces of meat, bell pepper and onion onto 8 skewers. Arrange the skewers on a roasting pan. |

| 9 | Grill the skewers for 6 to 8 minutes, turning them 4 times, as soon as the top side of the bell peppers is grilled. Squeeze the juice from the remaining lemon half on the skewers, if desired, and serve. |
|---|---|

**TIP**
❀

☛ If the orange bell pepper is difficult to find, you can leave it out. Red and yellow bell peppers are sufficient, but the result will be less colorful.

**SERVING SUGGESTION**
❀

Rice pilaf (see recipe 34) goes perfectly with these skewers.

5

# GARLIC CALAMARI

✤ YIELD: 4 SERVINGS • PREPARATION: 10 MINUTES • COOKING: 20 MINUTES ✤

2¼ pounds (1 kg) squid bodies (fresh or frozen)
2 garlic cloves
1 teaspoon (5 ml) olive oil

Salt & pepper, to taste
1 sprig cilantro
**NOTE:**
You'll need 4½ pounds (2 kg) whole squid to get 2¼ pounds (1 kg) squid bodies.

**PRELIMINARY:**
If the squid are frozen, thaw overnight in a large bowl in the refrigerator.

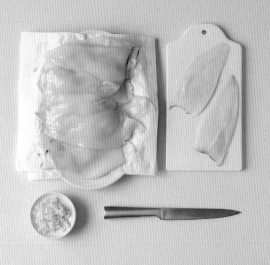

| 1 | Rinse the squid and let dry on paper towels. Cut each squid body in half or into quarters. Peel the garlic, remove the germs and mince the cloves. | 2 | Place the squid, garlic, oil, salt and pepper in a skillet. Cover and cook for 20 minutes over low heat. |
|---|---|---|---|
| 3 | Wash and dry the cilantro and pluck the leaves from the stems. Gather the leaves, roll them together tightly and mince. | 4 | Once the squid are cooked, remove from the heat, add the cilantro, mix and serve. |

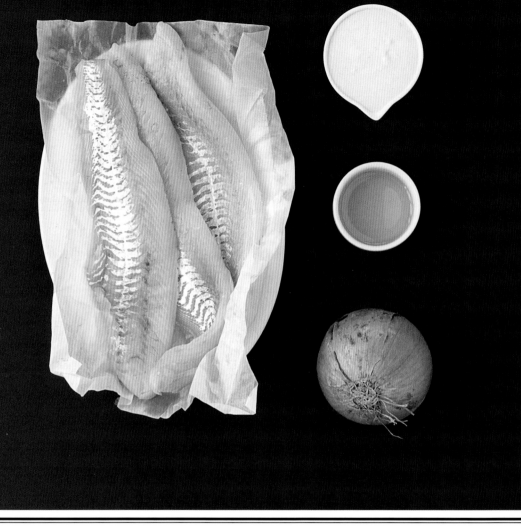

# POLLOCK WITH TARATOR SAUCE

**❧ YIELD: 4 SERVINGS • PREPARATION: 15 MINUTES • COOKING: 40 TO 50 MINUTES ❧**

1 large onion
2 tablespoons (30 ml) olive oil
1 pound (500 g) pollock fillets, cut into
   3 pieces

1 cup (250 ml) tarator sauce (see recipe 29)
Salt, to taste

**PRELIMINARY:**
Preheat the oven to 400°C (200°C).

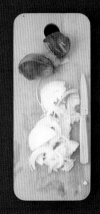

1 2
3 4

| | | | | |
|---|---|---|---|---|
| 1 | Peel the onion. Cut it in half and finely slice it. | 2 | Heat the olive oil in a skillet over medium heat and then sweat the onion over very low heat, covered. | |
| 3 | Once the onion is soft, take the lid off and let brown very lightly, stirring often. | 4 | Distribute the onion over the bottom of a baking dish the size of the pollock fillets. | ➤ |

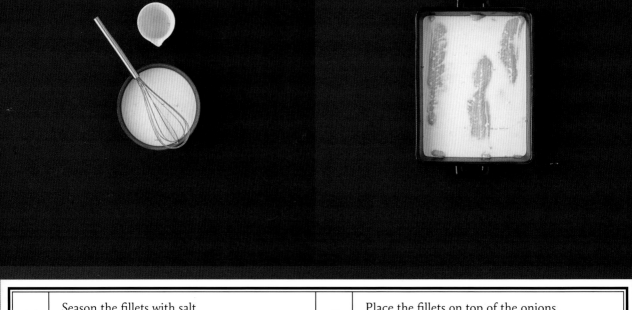

| 5 | Season the fillets with salt. | 6 | Place the fillets on top of the onions, overlapping if needed. |
|---|---|---|---|
| 7 | Mix the tarator sauce with about 1 to 2 cups (250 to 500 ml) water, adding as much water as needed to completely cover the pollock fillets with sauce. | 8 | Cover the fillets with the thinned tarator sauce, then place in the oven. Bake thinner fillets for 20 minutes and thicker fillets for 30 minutes. |

| 9 | Serve hot with a little or a lot of onion, according to taste, and with rice. |
|---|---|

**TIP**
❈

The next day, serve the cold leftovers with pitas.

**VARIATION**
❈

☛ You can substitute the white fish of your choice for the pollock fillets.

# STUFFED TROUT

❖ YIELD: 4 SERVINGS • PREPARATION: 20 MINUTES • MARINATING: 30 MINUTES • COOKING: 10 TO 12 MINUTES ❖

1 garlic clove
2 lemons
4 small trout
Salt & pepper, to taste

1 tablespoon (15 ml) ground walnuts
9 to 10 tablespoons (135 to 150 ml)
  ground sumac
2 tablespoons (30 ml) oil

**PRELIMINARY:**
Peel and cut the garlic in half. Juice the lemons. Rinse the fish and dry them with paper towels.

1 2
3 4

| | | | |
|---|---|---|---|
| 1 | Rub the skin of the fish with the garlic halves. Generously season the fish with salt and pepper. | 2 | Crush the garlic with a mortar and pestle. Mix the garlic with the ground walnuts and 1 heaping tablespoon (17 ml) sumac. |
| 3 | Stuff the trout with the garlic-sumac mixture and arrange them in a baking dish. Sprinkle the lemon juice on top and cover with the remaining sumac. Cover with plastic wrap and set aside in the refrigerator for 30 minutes. | 4 | Turn the oven's broiler on and place a rack at the top of the oven. Pour the oil over the fish and grill for 10 to 12 minutes, until the fish's skin browns. Serve. |

# MONKFISH TAGINE

❧ YIELD: 8 SERVINGS • PREPARATION: 50 MINUTES • INFUSION: 15 MINUTES • COOKING: 1 HOUR ❧

**FOR THE FISH STOCK:**
1 garlic clove
1⅓ ounces (40 g) flat-leaf parsley
2 tablespoons (30 ml) olive oil
Monkfish spine & sides (ask a fishmonger,
  as normally only the tails are available)

1 pinch saffron
1 teaspoon (5 ml) aniseeed
1 small pinch ras el hanout
**FOR THE TAGINE:**
1 tablespoon + 1 teaspoon (20 ml) olive oil
1 pinch saffron

1 pound (500 g) small new potatoes
4 tomatoes
1 onion
2 preserved lemons
3½ ounces (100 g) black olives
3½- pounds (1.5 kg) monkfish

| | | | | | |
|---|---|---|---|---|---|
| 1 | To make the stock, start by peeling and choping the garlic. Wash the parsley and knot the stems together to form a tight bunch. | 2 | Next heat the olive oil in a sauté pan or skillet over high heat and brown the spine and sides. | 3 | Add the garlic, mix and then add enough water to half-fill the pan. |
| 4 | Once the water boils, add the parsley, saffron, aniseed and ras el hanout. Simmer for 20 minutes. | 5 | Season with salt, pepper and let infuse for 15 minutes off the heat. Strain the stock through a fine-mesh strainer. | 6 | Rinse the sauté pan and return the stock to the pan. Simmer over medium heat. ➢ |

7 8
9 10

| | | | |
|---|---|---|---|
| 7 | To make the tagine, first mix 1 tablespoon (15 ml) of the olive oil and the saffron. | 8 | Peel the potatoes and cut horizontally into very thin slices. Dry them with paper towels and coat them with the saffron oil. |
| 9 | Peel the tomatoes (using a peeler for soft fruit and vegetables), cut into quarters and seed. | 10 | Peel the onion and slice it into thin rounds. |

11 12
13 14

| 11 | Slice the peel of one of the preserved lemons into 8 matchsticks. Cut the other preserved lemon into quarters. | 12 | Oil the bottom of a tagine with 1 teaspoon (5 ml) olive oil and layer first the potatoes, then the onion. | |
|---|---|---|---|---|
| 13 | Layer the tomatoes next and sprinkle the olives on top. | 14 | Add enough stock to reach the height of the potatoes, cover and cook over low heat for 15 minutes. | ➤ |

| 15 | Cut the monkfish into many pieces. Prick the flesh using a paring knife and insert a lemon matchstick into each slit. Arrange the monkfish on top of the olives and top the monkfish with the preserved lemon quarters. Continue cooking for 45 minutes to 1 hour. | **TIP**<br>❋<br><br>Insist that your fishmonger remove all the red and brown flesh from the monkfish, as well as the translucent "skins." Indeed, this is not an easy thing to do yourself, and they shrink during cooking. They will also make the monkfish taste less pleasing. |

| 16 | Serve the tagine in its own dish. | **VARIATION**<br>❋<br><br>You can substitute another fish for the monkfish, but the cooking will likely take less time, as the pieces of monkfish are thick. |

# FISH BASTILLA

**✦ YIELD: 4 SERVINGS • PREPARATION: 1 HOUR • MARINATING: 30 MINUTES • COOKING: 30 TO 35 MINUTES ✦**

1⅓ ounces (40 g) cilantro
1⅓ ounces (40 g) flat-leaf parsley
2 garlic cloves
1 lemon
½ teaspoon (2 ml) mild chili powder

Salt, to taste
½ teaspoon (2 ml) ground cumin
3 tablespoons (45 ml) red wine vinegar
⅓ cup (75 ml) olive oil
1 pound (500 g) white fish fillet

3½ ounces (100 g) soy vermicelli
3 tablespoons (45 ml) butter
6 sheets brik or phyllo pastry
1 tablespoon (15 ml) confectioners' sugar

1 2
3 4

| | | | |
|---|---|---|---|
| 1 | Wash and dry the cilantro and parsley. Chop off the stems just below the leaves. | 2 | Peel the garlic cloves, cut in half and remove the germs. Zest and juice the lemon. |
| 3 | Place the garlic, chili powder and 1 large pinch salt in the bowl of a food processor. Puree well. Add the cumin, cilantro and parsley. Blend until you obtain a smooth paste. | 4 | Add the lemon juice, vinegar and olive oil to the puree and mix using a fork. Add half the zest. Divide this mixture in half. ➢ |

5 6
7 8

| 5 | Place the fish in a bowl and coat with half the herb mixture. Cover and set aside for ½ hour in the refrigerator. | 6 | Bring a saucepan of water to a boil. Turn the heat off and add the vermicelli. Cover, leave for 5 minutes and then drain and rinse with water. |
|---|---|---|---|
| 7 | Heat a little olive oil in a non-stick skillet over medium-high heat. Add the fish fillet and cook for 3 to 8 minutes, depending on the thickness. Turn over once if the fillet is thick. | 8 | Take the pan off the heat and add the drained vermicelli. Mix carefully. Sprinkle the rest of the lemon zest on top. Transfer to a bowl and let cool. |

9 10
11 12

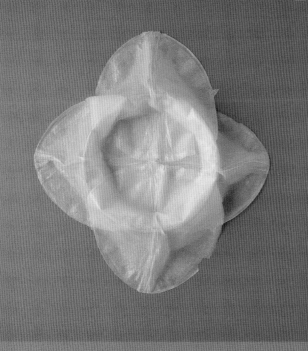

| 9 | Preheat the oven to 400°F (200°C). Melt the butter. Stack the sheets of brik pastry and brush the top one with melted butter. Place the buttered pastry sheet in the center of a deep cake pan or a round baking dish. | 10 | Repeat with a second buttered pastry sheet, placing it on top of the first one. Place a third buttered pastry sheet straddling the pan and the work surface. | |
|---|---|---|---|---|
| 11 | Repeat with the last 3 pastry sheets, buttering them and arranging them in a rosette pattern around the pan. | 12 | Add the fish and vermicelli filling to the center of the pastry-lined pan and cover with the remaining herb mixture. | ➤ |

13 Fold the pastry sheets over to seal the bastilla. Tuck any edges that stick out into the pan, around the edge of the bastilla. Sprinkle water overtop to keep the pastry from curling while it cooks. Bake for 10 to 15 minutes, until the pastry is crispy and golden.

| | |
|---|---|
| 14 | Preheat the oven's broiler and place a rack at the top of the oven. Sprinkle the entire surface of the bastilla with confectioners' sugar and caramelize under the broiler for a few seconds. To turn the bastilla out of the pan, begin by lifting it with a spatula to see if it will come out easily. If this is the case, take a second spatula, lift and take the bastilla out of the pan. |

**TURNING OUT**
❋

☛ Turning out the bastilla is not easy because you risk puncturing it while you're handling it. You can serve the bastilla in the pan in which you cooked it. If you're skillful, you can turn out the bastilla by placing a plate on top, turning the bastilla over and then turning it back over into its serving dish (you turn the bastilla over twice so it will be right side up in the dish).

# FISH WITH CHERMOULA SAUCE

➤ **YIELD: 6 SERVINGS** • PREPARATION: 20 MINUTES • MARINATING: 30 MINUTES • COOKING: 3 TO 8 MINUTES ◄

1⅓ ounces (40 g) cilantro
1⅓ ounces (40 g) flat-leaf parsley
2 garlic cloves
1 lemon
Salt, to taste

½ teaspoon (2 ml) mild chili powder
½ teaspoon (2 ml) ground cumin
3 tablespoons (45 ml) red wine vinegar
⅓ cup (75 ml) olive oil
1½ pounds (650 g) white fish fillets

**PRELIMINARY:**
Wash and dry the cilantro and parsley.

1 2
3 4

| | | | |
|---|---|---|---|
| 1 | Chop the stems of the cilantro and parsley off just below the leaves. Peel the garlic cloves. Zest and juice the lemon. | 2 | Slice the garlic cloves in half and remove the germ. In a food processor, blend the garlic, 1 large pinch salt and the chili powder. Puree well. |
| 3 | Add the cumin and cilantro and parsley leaves. Blend until you obtain a smooth paste. | 4 | Add the lemon juice, half the lemon zest, the vinegar and 4½ tablespoons (67 ml) olive oil, and mix the chermoula with a fork. ➢ |

5 6
7 8

| 5 | Divide the chermoula in half. | 6 | Place the fish fillets in a bowl and coat with half the chermoula. Cover and set aside for ½ hour in the refrigerator. |
|---|---|---|---|
| 7 | Heat the rest of the olive oil in a non-stick skillet over medium-high heat. Add the fish fillets and cook for 3 to 8 minutes, depending on the thickness. | 8 | Turn over once, unless the fillets are so thin they can cook through without being turned over. |

| 9 | Cover the fish with the remaining chermoula, sprinkle the remaining lemon zest on top and serve. | **TIP** ❋ <br> ☛ This dish is also delicious served cold. |
|---|---|---|

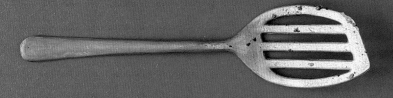

# BREAM WITH HOT ESCABECHE SAUCE

❧ **YIELD: 4 SERVINGS** • PREPARATION: 10 MINUTES • COOKING: 7 TO 10 MINUTES ❧

1 red onion
6 tablespoons (90 ml) olive oil
1 pound (500 g) bream fillets
⅓ cup (75 ml) raisins

¼ cup (60 ml) pine nuts
½ teaspoon (2 ml) ground cinnamon
7 tablespoons (105 ml) red wine vinegar

**PRELIMINARY:**
Peel the onion, slice it in half and then mince it.

1 2
3 4

| 1 | Heat 2 tablespoons (30 ml) oil in a non-stick skillet over medium-high heat and cook the bream fillets for 3 to 5 minutes, depending on the thickness. Transfer the fillets to a dish and set aside. | 2 | Place the onion, raisins, pine nuts and cinnamon in the skillet. Brown, stirring regularly, for 2 minutes. |
|---|---|---|---|
| 3 | Add the vinegar. Bring to a boil and let the vinegar evaporate. | 4 | Pour the sauce over the fish fillets and then drizzle on the remaining olive oil. Serve. |

## 6

## TEA

## DESSERTS

# MINT TEA

✦ **YIELD: 1 POT** • PREPARATION: 10 MINUTES • COOKING: 5 MINUTES • INFUSION : 8 TO 13 MINUTES ✦

⅔ ounce (20 g) mint
3 cups (750 ml) water
1 tablespoon (15 ml) gunpowder green tea
¼ cup (60 ml) sugar

**PRELIMINARY:**
Wash the mint and remove the lower part
of the stems. Bring the water to a boil.

**TIP:**
The longer you steep the tea, the stronger
the taste will be; otherwise the taste of the
mint will dominate.

1
2
3
4
5
6

| | | | | | |
|---|---|---|---|---|---|
| 1 | Pour a little boiling water into a teapot and move the pot in a circular motion. Discard the water. | 2 | Put the tea in a bowl, cover with boiling water and ser aside for 1 minute (to let the leaves open up). | 3 | Strain the tea and discard the water. Put the tea in the teapot. |
| 4 | Add the mint, twisting the stems and leaves to enhance their flavor, and then add the sugar. | 5 | Cover with boiling water and let steep for 3 minutes, without mixing. | 6 | Mix the tea by filling a glass and pouring the tea back into the pot 2 or 3 times. Let steep another 5 to 10 minutes, to taste. |

# GLAZED BEIGNETS

✦ **YIELD: 20 BEIGNETS** • PREPARATION: 15 MINUTES • RESTING: 30 MINUTES • COOKING: 20 MINUTES ✦

1⅛ cups (280 ml) sheep's milk yogurt
1 cup (250 ml) flour
½ teaspoon (2 ml) baking soda
6 tablespoons (90 ml) water

1⅓ cups (325 ml) confectioners' sugar
1 tablespoon (15 ml) orange blossom water
Oil, for frying

| | | | | | |
|---|---|---|---|---|---|
| 1 | Mix the yogurt, flour and baking soda using a spatula. | 2 | Let rest for 30 minutes at room temperature. | 3 | Bring the water and sugar to a boil. Lower the heat and let simmer for 10 minutes. |
| 4 | Once the syrup is ready, take the pan off the heat and add the orange blossom water. Mix. | 5 | Place spoonfuls of dough into the hot oil and fry for 5 minutes, until golden. | 6 | Dip the hot beignets into the syrup. Coat the balls well and take them out using a skimmer. |

# BAKLAVA

**❖ YIELD: 15 TO 20 PIECES • PREPARATION: 40 MINUTES • COOKING: 2½ HOURS ❖**

½ cup (125 ml) butter
4½ ounces (125 g) walnuts
  (about 1 cup/250 ml)
4½ ounces (125 g) blanched almonds
  (about ¾ cup/175 ml)

⅓ cup (75 ml) sugar
1 teaspoon (5 ml) ground cinnamon
20 sheets brik or phyllo pastry
**FOR THE SYRUP:**
1 lemon
1 scant cup (230 ml) water

⅓ cup (75 ml) sugar
6 tablespoons (90 ml) honey
**PRELIMINARY:**
Preheat the oven to 300°F (150°C) and
place a rack in the middle and a drip pan
underneath. Melt the butter.

1 2
3 4

| 1 | Process the walnuts and almonds in a food processor until you obtain a fairly fine powder. Mix the powdered nuts with the sugar and cinnamon. | 2 | Stack the pastry sheets on a board. Place a baking dish on the sheets and cut the pastry to fit the bottom of the pan. | |
|---|---|---|---|---|
| 3 | Arrange 6 sheets in the bottom of the pan, brushing each with butter as you work. | 4 | Sprinkle a third of the nut mixture overtop. Place 2 buttered pastry sheets on top and sprinkle another third of the nut mixture overtop. | ➢ |

5 6
7 8

| 5 | Repeat with 2 more buttered pastry sheets and the rest of the nut mixture. Place 10 buttered pastry sheets on top. Bring a small saucepan of water to a boil. | 6 | Cut a diamond-shaped pattern into the baklava. Pour the saucepan of water into the drip pan and place the baklava in the oven. Bake for 2 hours, until golden. |
|---|---|---|---|
| 7 | As soon as the baklava is in the oven, prepare the syrup: using a peeler, remove a strip of zest from the lemon. Juice the lemon. | 8 | Heat the water, sugar, lemon zest and 1 teaspoon (5 ml) lemon juice. Whisk while bringing the mixture to a boil. Lower the heat and let simmer for 15 minutes. Add the honey and simmer for 5 minutes. Remove the zest. |

9 Take the baklava out of the oven and pour the cooled syrup over the hot baklava. Serve warm or hot.

**TIP**
❋

☛ Lightly sprinkle a little water on top of the baklava just before putting it in the oven to keep the pastry sheets from curling while it bakes. To do this, moisten your fingers and throw water droplets onto the pastry.

# TURKISH DELIGHT

**⊰ YIELD: 25 SMALL CANDIES • PREPARATION: 15 MINUTES • RESTING: 3 HOURS • COOKING: 35 TO 40 MINUTES ⊱**

2 lemons
⅔ cup + 1 tablespoon (165 ml) cornstarch
1 scant cup (230 ml) water
2 cups (500 ml) granulated sugar
2 tablespoons (30 ml) rose water

About 4 drops red food coloring or 1 teaspoon (5 ml) beet juice
2 tablespoons (30 ml) confectioners' sugar

**PRELIMINARY:**
Line a square or rectangular mold or baking dish with parchment paper. Juice the lemons.

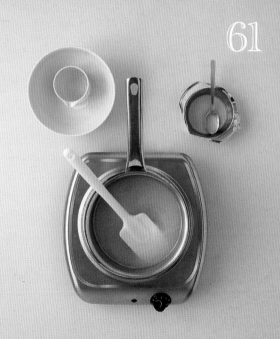

1  2
3  4

| 1 | Mix ⅔ cup (150 ml) cornstarch into 7 tablespoons (105 ml) water. | 2 | Pour 8½ tablespoons (127 ml) water, 1 teaspoon (5 ml) lemon juice and the granulated sugar into a saucepan. Place over medium heat and mix with a spatula to dissolve the sugar. | |
|---|---|---|---|---|
| 3 | Bring the mixture to a boil and boil until the syrup thickens, becomes viscous and bubbles stick to the spatula. The syrup must not brown. | 4 | Take the pan off the heat, add the lemon juice and mix. Stir the cornstarch mixture again, in the bowl, and mix it into the syrup. | ➤ |

5 6
7 8

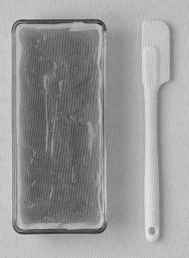

| 5 | Bring the syrup mixture to a boil and cook for 20 to 25 minutes over medium heat, stirring constantly. The mixture should not be releasing any steam. | 6 | When it becomes difficult to continue stirring the mixture, add the rose water, then the food coloring, and stir until you obtain an even texture. |
|---|---|---|---|
| 7 | Pour into the prepared mold or dish, smooth the surface using an oiled spatula and let cool. | 8 | Cover a plate with a mixture of confectioners' sugar and 1 tablespoon (15 ml) cornstarch. When the Turkish delight is at room temperature, turn it out of the mold and onto the plate. Coat with the sugar mixture. |

| 9 | Cut into cubes using scissors, coating each side with the sugar mixture. |
|---|---|

**TIP**
※

☛ If you don't want too much confectioners' sugar on the Turkish delight, you can place them in a strainer and shake them to remove any excess.

**COOKING TIP**
※

The Turkish delight paste is ready when it looks like a mass that can be lifted in one piece using a spatula.

# ALMOND BRIOUATS (PASTRY TRIANGLES)

### ❧ YIELD: 16 BRIOUATS • PREPARATION: 30 MINUTES • COOKING: 8 TO 12 MINUTES ❧

1½ cups (375 ml) ground almonds
¼ cup (60 ml) sugar
½ teaspoon (2 ml) ground cinnamon

1 teaspoon (5 ml) orange blossom water
2 teaspoons (10 ml) butter, cut into pieces
1 small egg white

4 sheets brik or phyllo pastry
2 cups (500 ml) oil, for frying
7 tablespoons (105 ml) honey

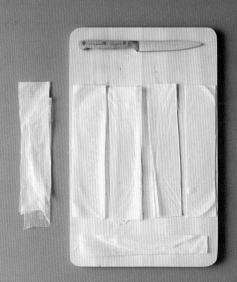

1 2
3 4

| 1 | Whisk together the ground almonds, sugar, cinnamon and orange blossom water in a large bowl. | 2 | Add the butter and incorporate it into the almond mixture by rubbing it between your fingers. | |
|---|---|---|---|---|
| 3 | Add the egg white and knead until the dough is uniform (about 1 minute). | 4 | Stack the pastry sheets (without removing the parchment paper lining them). If the sheets are circular, square them off by trimming the ends with a knife. Cut the sheets into 4 rectangular strips. | ➤ |

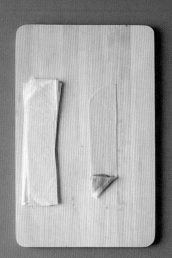

5 6
7 8

| 5 | Stack the strips one on top of the other. Take a strip, peel off the paper and place 1 heaping teaspoon (6 ml) filling at the edge. | 6 | Fold the pastry at a right angle over the filling. Flatten the filling a little and continue folding at right angles, forming a triangle. |
|---|---|---|---|
| 7 | Tuck the end of the pastry into the last fold, like an envelope. | 8 | Heat the oil in a large skillet and fry the briouats for 2 to 3 minutes, until golden. Take the pastries out of the oil using a skimmer and drain on paper towels. |

| 9 | Melt the honey in a saucepan over medium heat. Once the honey is liquid, take the saucepan off the heat and drop the briouats into the honey. Soak with honey by turning them over 1 or 2 times. Drain on a wire rack. | **TIP**<br>❋<br>For a less sweet result, leave out the honey. |
|---|---|---|

# GAZELLE HORNS

❧ YIELD: 15 PASTRIES • PREPARATION: 40 MINUTES • RESTING: 1 HOUR • COOKING: 15 MINUTES ❧

**FOR THE DOUGH:**
1⅜ cup (340 ml) flour
1 pinch salt
1 egg, beaten

3½ tablespoons (52 ml) neutral oil (such as grapeseed, canola or sunflower)
2 tablespoons (30 ml) orange blossom water
**FOR THE FILLING:**
3 cups (750 ml) ground almonds

1 teaspoon (5 ml) ground cinnamon
6½ tablespoons (97 ml) sugar
3 tablespoons (45 ml) orange blossom water
1½ tablespoons (22 ml) butter, softened & cut into pieces

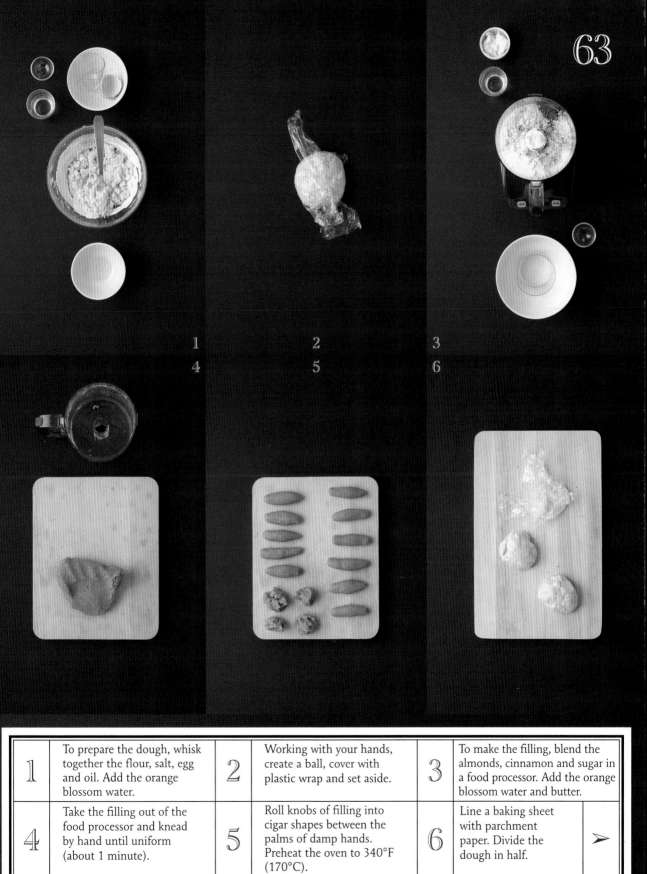

|   |   |   |   |
|---|---|---|---|
| 1 | To prepare the dough, whisk together the flour, salt, egg and oil. Add the orange blossom water. | 2 | Working with your hands, create a ball, cover with plastic wrap and set aside. |
| 4 | Take the filling out of the food processor and knead by hand until uniform (about 1 minute). | 5 | Roll knobs of filling into cigar shapes between the palms of damp hands. Preheat the oven to 340°F (170°C). |

|   |   |
|---|---|
| 3 | To make the filling, blend the almonds, cinnamon and sugar in a food processor. Add the orange blossom water and butter. |
| 6 | Line a baking sheet with parchment paper. Divide the dough in half. ➤ |

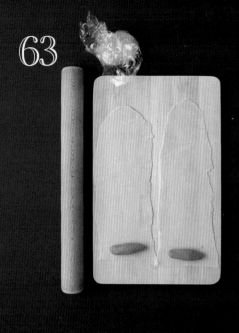

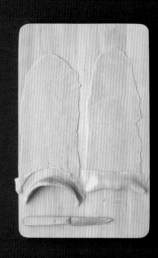

7 8
9 10

| 7 | Roll out one of the pastry balls on a floured surface, creating a thin rectangle. Cut the rectangle in half. Place 1 cigar of filling on the edge of the pastry. | 8 | Fold the bottom of the strip over the filling and seal, pressing with your fingertips. |
|---|---|---|---|
| 9 | Flatten the pastry by pressing it between your fingers and shape it into a crescent. Seal the ends. Trim any excess pastry. | 10 | Arrange the pastries on a baking sheet. When the first ball of dough is used up, roll out the second ball and continue until all the filling has been used. |

| 11 | Bake for 15 minutes. Let the horns cool before removing them from the baking sheet. | STORAGE<br>❁<br>Gazelle horns can be stored in a sealed container. |
|---|---|---|
| **TECHNIQUE**<br>❁ | | **VARIATION**<br>❁ |
| By rolling the knobs of filling between the palms of your hands, you naturally get a small cigar shape that's a little thicker in the middle than at the ends. | | Once the horns have chilled, you can lightly brush them with orange blossom water, then sprinkle a little confectioners' sugar overtop. |

# DATE MA'AMOUL

❖ **YIELD: 20 COOKIES** • **PREPARATION: 50 MINUTES** • **COOKING: 20 TO 25 MINUTES** ❖

7¾ ounces (220 g) dates
⅔ cup (150 ml) butter
1¼ cups (425 ml) cake & pastry flour

1 or 2 tablespoons (15 to 30 ml) orange
  blossom water
1 to 3 tablespoons (15 to 45 ml) milk
Confectioners' sugar, for dusting

**PRELIMINARY:**
Preheat the oven to 300°F (150°C). Line a
baking sheet with parchment paper.

1
4

2
5

3
6

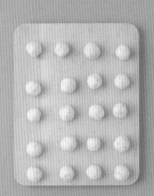

| 1 | Pit the dates. Cut into quarters using an oiled knife. | 2 | Melt 2½ tablespoons (37 ml) butter in a saucepan and add the date pieces. | 3 | Stir and cook over low heat until the dates are easy to crush and form a paste. | |
|---|---|---|---|---|---|---|
| 4 | Put the flour in a bowl and incorporate the remaining butter using your fingertips. | 5 | Gradually add the orange blossom water and milk until the dough comes together, then knead until it is supple. | 6 | Divide the dough into 20 pieces and roll in the palms of your hands to form 20 balls. | ➢ |

7 8
9 10

| 7 | Divide the date paste into 20 pieces and form 20 balls. | 8 | Flatten the dough balls between the palms of your hands and place a ball of date paste in the center of each dough disk. |
|---|---|---|---|
| 9 | Seal the dough over the filling and press to seal. Form balls and place them on the baking sheet. | 10 | Flatten the balls by pressing the tines of a fork into each one. Bake for 20 to 25 minutes. The cookies must not brown. |

| 11 | Let the cookies cool on the baking sheet, then dust with confectioners' sugar. |
|---|---|

### STORAGE
❀

The cookies can be stored in a sealed container.

### BAKING
❀

Baking these cookies is a delicate operation because they must not brown. You have to touch them to know when they're done. Tap the surface of one of the cookies after 20 to 25 minutes of baking (sooner if your oven cooks hot): the cookie should resist the pressure a little. If it is soft, continue baking for 5 minutes, then test again.

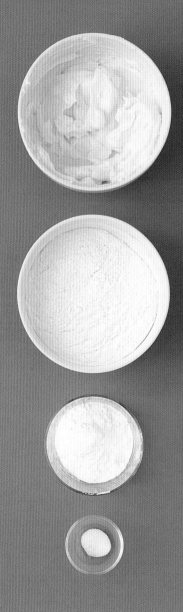

# GHORAYEBAH

❧ **YIELD: 10 COOKIES** • **PREPARATION: 20 MINUTES** • **COOKING: 20 MINUTES** ❧

1 cup + 3 tablespoons (295 ml) cake & pastry flour
2 tablespoons (30 ml) confectioners' sugar

7 tablespoons (105 ml) butter, softened
1 pinch salt
Confectioners sugar, for coating

**PRELIMINARY:**
Preheat the oven to 350°F (180°C). Line a baking sheet with parchment paper.

1 2
3 4

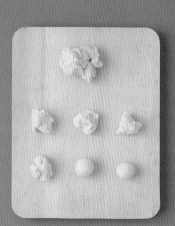

| 1 | Sift the flour and confectioners' sugar separately by passing them through a fine-mesh strainer. | 2 | Using an electric mixer, cream the softened butter with the confectioners' sugar and salt until the mixture is pale and fluffy. | |
|---|---|---|---|---|
| 3 | Add the flour in 3 batches, mixing it in by hand. | 4 | Divide the dough into 10 pieces and roll into 10 balls between the palms of your hands. | ➤ |

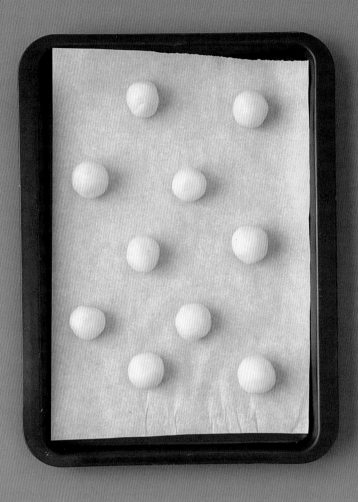

| 5 | Arrange the balls of dough on the baking sheet. Bake for 20 minutes (the cookies will flatten slightly on their own). | **SOFTENED BUTTER: BASIC METHOD**<br>❋<br>To soften butter, you have to first cut it into small pieces and then let it sit at room temperature for 20 minutes to 2 hours, depending on the room's temperature. The butter is ready when you can sink a finger into it easily. |

| | |
|---|---|
| 6 | Let the cookies cool before coating them in confectioners' sugar. |

**STORAGE**
❋

These cookies can be stored in a sealed container.

**SOFTENED BUTTER: EXPRESS METHOD**
❋

Bring a small saucepan of water to a boil and take it off the heat. Put the pieces of butter in a heat-resistant bowl and set the bowl in the saucepan. Leave the bowl for a few seconds, then take it out of the saucepan and work the butter with a spatula until it's soft.

# CUSTARD BASTILLA

❧ YIELD: 4 SERVINGS • PREPARATION: 35 MINUTES • COOKING: 30 MINUTES ❧

1 orange
1 scant cup (230 ml) milk
1 cinnamon stick
1 heaping teaspoon (6 ml) cornstarch
1 egg yolk
2 tablespoons (30 ml) confectioners' sugar

4 sheets brik or phyllo pastry
¼ cup (60 ml) butter, melted
⅓ cup (75 ml) brown sugar
2 ounces (60 g) blanched almonds (about ⅜ cup/90 ml)
3 tablespoons (45 ml) honey

**PRELIMINARY:**
Preheat the oven to 400°F (200°C). Line a baking sheet with parchment paper.

1 2
3 4

| 1 | Zest half the orange. | 2 | Infuse all but 2 tablespoons (30 ml) of the milk, the orange zest and the cinnamon stick in a saucepan over low heat for 10 minutes. | |
|---|---|---|---|---|
| 3 | Using a fork, mix the cornstarch with 2 tablespoons (30 ml) milk. | 4 | Whisk the egg yolk and confectioners' sugar until the mixture becomes pale. | ➤ |

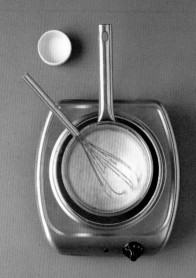

5 6
7 8

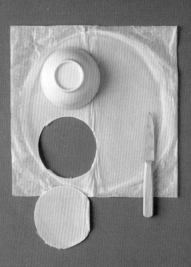

| | | | |
|---|---|---|---|
| 5 | Bring the milk to a boil, remove the cinnamon stick and then whisk the mixture into the sugar and egg yolk. | 6 | Pour the milk–egg yolk mixture into the saucepan and simmer. Pour in the mixed cornstarch and whisk over medium heat until thickened. |
| 7 | Once the sauce thickens, pour it into a bowl and place plastic wrap directly on top, touching the sauce. Refrigerate. | 8 | Stack the pastry sheets (without removing the parchment paper lining). Using a knife, cut out 4 disks about 4 inches (10 cm) in diameter (to create 16 pastry disks). |

9 10
11 12

| 9 | Stack these disks one on top of the other. Take a pastry disk, peel off the parchment paper and brush with melted butter. | 10 | Sprinkle brown sugar onto the buttered pastry disk and repeat with 5, 6 or 7 disks, depending on the size of the baking sheet. Arrange the disks on the sheet. | |
|---|---|---|---|---|
| 11 | Bake about 5 minutes, until golden. Take the pastry disks out of the oven and remove them from the baking sheet. Repeat with the remaining pastry disks. | 12 | Toast the almonds in a dry skillet (without any fat) over medium-high heat, stirring often. | ➤ |

13 14
15 16

| 13 | Take the almonds out of the skillet and coarsely chop. | 14 | Once the sauce has cooled and just before serving, melt the honey in a small saucepan over low heat. |
|----|----|----|----|
| 15 | Arrange a pastry sheet on each plate. Add a thin layer of sauce with a spoon and sprinkle almonds on top. | 16 | Repeat twice, to add 2 more layers of pastry and sauce. |

| 17 | Finish with a buttered pastry sheet, sprinkle almonds on top and pour melted honey over each bastilla. Serve. | **TIP** ❀ <br> ☞ Mixing cornstarch into a boiling liquid can create lumps. To avoid this, it's better to whisk in the starch while the liquid is hot but not boiling and, especially, to whisk constantly! |

# DATE & WALNUT CAKE

**⋟ YIELD: 8 TO 10 SERVINGS • PREPARATION: 25 MINUTES • COOKING: 45 TO 50 MINUTES ⋞**

7½ tablespoons (112 ml) butter + extra to
  butter the dish
5 ounces (150 g) dates
3½ ounces (100 g) walnuts
2½ cups + 2 tablespoons (655 ml) all-
  purpose or bread flour
1 teaspoon (5 ml) baking soda

½ teaspoon (2 ml) salt
1 tablespoon (15 ml) ground ginger
1 teaspoon (5 ml) ground allspice
1 teaspoon (5 ml) ground cinnamon
1 teaspoon (5 ml) ground nutmeg
7 tablespoons (105 ml) milk
½ cup (125 ml) plain yogurt

1 egg
¾ cup (175 ml) sugar
¾ cup (175 ml) honey
**PRELIMINARY:** Preheat the oven to
350°F (180°C).

1 2
3 4

| 1 | Melt the 7½ tablespoons (112 ml) butter. Butter a rectangular baking dish. | 2 | Pit the dates and cut them into small pieces. Oil the blade of the knife to keep the dates from sticking to the blade. | |
|---|---|---|---|---|
| 3 | Break the walnuts into small pieces between your fingers. | 4 | Mix the 2½ cups (625 ml) flour, baking soda, salt, ginger, allspice, cinnamon and nutmeg in a bowl. | ➤ |

5 6
7 8

| 5 | If the milk is cold, warm it in a large saucepan over low heat. Add the yogurt and egg. Whisk and take the pan off the heat. (The goal is to warm cold ingredients, not to cook them.) | 6 | Add the sugar, honey and melted butter. Whisk to completely mix the ingredients. |
|---|---|---|---|
| 7 | Mix the dates with 2 tablespoons (30 ml) flour so they don't stick together. | 8 | Add the dry ingredients to the milk mixture and whisk until they are completely mixed. Add the dates and walnuts halfway through. |

| 9 | Pour the batter into the dish and bake for 45 to 50 minutes, until the cake is golden and the blade of a knife comes out clean from the center. | **STORAGE**<br>❄<br>Wrapped in plastic wrap, this cake can be stored at room temperature for 5 days. |

# RICE PUDDING

❧ **YIELD: 8 TO 10 SERVINGS** • PREPARATION: 10 MINUTES • COOKING: 50 MINUTES • RESTING: 2 HOURS ❧

½ cup (250 ml) short-grain rice
1¼ cups (310 ml) water
1 quart (1 L) whole milk

3 tablespoons (45 ml) cornstarch
½ cup (125 ml) confectioners' sugar
2 tablespoons (30 ml) orange blossom water

**PRELIMINARY:**
Rinse the rice. Pour it and the water into a saucepan.

| | | | | | |
|---|---|---|---|---|---|
| 1 | Bring the rice to a boil. Cook for 30 minutes over low heat. Once the water has been absorbed, stop cooking. | 2 | Set aside ½ cup (125 ml) of milk and bring the rest to a boil in a large saucepan. | 3 | Pour the reserved milk onto the cornstarch and mix using a fork. |
| 4 | Add the cornstarch mixture to the hot milk and then add the rice. Bring to a boil again, stirring. | 5 | Take the pan off the heat and add the sugar and orange blossom water. Whisk. | 6 | Pour the pudding into a bowl, cover partially and let cool. Refrigerate for 2 hours. |

# GLAZED ORANGES

➤ **YIELD: 4 SERVINGS** • PREPARATION: 20 MINUTES • COOKING: 2 MINUTES • RESTING: 1 HOUR ➤

7 oranges
¼ cup (60 ml) sugar (2 tablespoons/30 ml)
   if the oranges are very sweet)
1 cinnamon stick

2 tablespoons (30 ml) orange blossom water
1 sprig mint, washed, dried & the leaves
   plucked from the stem

**TIP:** To go a little faster, place the orange slices, orange-cinnamon syrup and orange blossom water in a serving bowl. Cover, refrigerate and then serve with the chopped mint.

| | | | | | |
|---|---|---|---|---|---|
| 1 | Zest 1 orange and juice 3 oranges. Place the zest in a small saucepan, then add the juice. | 2 | Add the sugar and cinnamon stick to the orange zest and juice. Bring to a boil, stirring. Take off the heat and let infuse. | 3 | Cut off the ends of the remaining 4 oranges, then peel them with a knife. |
| 4 | Cut the oranges into thin slices and arrange the slices in a rosette pattern on 4 plates. | 5 | Add the orange blossom water to the juice mixture. Pour the mixture over the oranges, cover and refrigerate for 1 hour. | 6 | Mince the mint just before serving. Distribute the mint over each plate. |

# MOUHALABIEH

❧ **YIELD: 4 SERVINGS • PREPARATION: 20 MINUTES • COOKING: 10 MINUTES • RESTING: 2 HOURS** ❦

4½ tablespoons (67 ml) cornstarch
2 cups (500 ml) milk
½ cup (125 ml) sugar
2 tablespoons (30 ml) rose water

2 tablespoons (30 ml) orange blossom water
1 ounce (20 g) blanched almonds (about 3
tablespoons/45 ml)

1 ounce (20 g) shelled pistachios
(about 3 tablespoons/45 ml)

| 1 | Mix the cornstarch with 7 tablespoons (105 ml) milk. | 2 | Bring the remaining milk to a boil. Lower the heat, add the sugar, then the cornstarch, and mix. | 3 | Take the pan off the heat. Add the rose water and orange blossom water, then mix. |
| 4 | Pour into 4 ramekins. Let cool, cover and refrigerate for 2 hours. | 5 | Crush the almonds and pistachios. Toast the nuts in a dry skillet. | 6 | Serve the mouhalabieh with the crushed pistachios and almonds sprinkled on top. |

# INGREDIENTS AND CULINARY TERMS

# GEOGRAPHIC ORIGINS

# TABLE OF CONTENTS

# INDEX OF RECIPES

# THEMATIC INDEX

# ACKNOWLEDGMENTS

# INGREDIENTS AND CULINARY TERMS

**ALLSPICE**

The whole or ground berries of *Pimenta officinalis*, allspice takes its name from the fact that it tastes like a combination of cinnamon, nutmeg and cloves, not because it's a spice blend containing various spices.

**BLANCH**

To blanch means to plunge into boiling water for a few seconds, then plunge into cold water to stop the cooking. It is usually done to remove the skin of a fruit, vegetable or nut (tomato, peach, almond, pistachio). However, since the invention of soft fruit and vegetable peelers, blanching is no longer essential for removing the skins of tomatoes, peaches and the like (or peppers, which need to be broiled if the skins are going to be peeled off by hand). If, however, you don't have a soft fruit peeler, you can leave the skin on the tomatoes for all the recipes contained in this book, except for oven-roasted tomatoes.

**BRIK PASTRY**

Made of semolina boiled in water and then cooked in olive oil, brik pastry sheets are easy to use as long as you don't let them dry out. To keep them from drying out, store them in their original packaging and keep them stacked one on top of the other. Do not peel off the parchment paper that lines the sheet until you're ready to use it. Brik pastry sheets are not as readily available as phyllo, which is available in the frozen foods section of most large supermarkets. Look for brik pastry in Middle Eastern and other specialty food stores.

**BULGUR**

Wheat that has been cooked, dried and crushed. When it's simply called "bulgur," and no size is specified, it's considered "coarse," which requires cooking. The type used to make tabbouleh and kibbeh is "fine" bulgur, which does not require cooking. You can sometimes find fine bulgur in supermarkets, but you're more likely to find it in health food stores or specialty food stores.

**COOKING TIMES**

The cooking times indicated in this book are suggestions only. Indeed, one oven can function differently from another, some broilers only heat intermittently and "medium heat" can also vary greatly from one burner to another. Therefore, you always need to keep on eye on how the cooking is progressing.

**COUSCOUS**

The couscous available at most supermarkets is considered "instant" couscous. Prepare it by putting the couscous in a heat-resistant bowl, adding an equal part of boiling water and leaving the couscous to absorb the water, off the heat. It will cook in about five minutes.

**DEGLAZE**

Heating and stirring a small amount of liquid, such as wine or stock, in a pan in which other foods, usually meat, have been cooked. Done to dissolve small food particles stuck to the bottom of the pan.

**FRYING**

You know the oil is at the right temperature to deep fry or shallow fry when the food begins to sizzle as soon as it's placed in the oil. It must not, however, start to brown right away. If it turns golden immediately, the oil is too hot.

**GARLIC**

Some garlic cloves, because of their age, have a large germ inside. This should be removed because it can add bitterness to the dish. To do this, you simply need to cut the garlic clove in half and remove the germ with the tip of a knife. In many instances, the recipes in this book call for garlic cloves to then be crushed. You can crush garlic either with a garlic press or a mortar and pestle. You can also use the method used in restaurants: cut the garlic clove in half, lay it on a flat work surface place the flat edge of a chef's knife (which has a wide, thick blade) on top and hit the flat edge of the knife with your fist. The garlic clove will be smashed flat, and you can then easily chop it very finely.

**HERBS**

Middle Eastern cooking is rich in herbs: flat-leaf parsley, cilantro and mint can be found in almost all dishes. To prepare them, you must first rinse them and then dry them. Drying is especially important for mint, which blackens when it remains wet and exposed to the air (i.e., not submerged). When you have to cut a large amount of parsley or cilantro, gather the herbs into an organized bunch, to be able to separate the leaves from the stems. Discard the stems, tightly pack the leaves together and mince as finely as possible with a sharp knife. Unfortunately, there is no shortcut for mint, and it takes time to carefully pluck the leaves from the stems.

**KNIVES**

Middle Eastern cooking requires the use of a lot of knives! Many mixtures (especially those involving raw vegetables) must be finely minced. To do this, it's essential to have a set of sharp knives. These make the work a lot easier and more precise, and it's the only way (aside from wearing swimming goggles) to not cry while cutting onions. A dull knife crushes the onion, thus causing its juices to escape, which is what makes your eyes water.

### LAMB

Lamb is the meat most used in Middle Eastern cooking. The shoulder is the ideal cut for cooking dishes that simmer for a long time. (For the recipes in this book, you'll need to ask your butcher to completely debone the shoulder). The leg is a good all-purpose cut, suitable for short and long cooking times. If you intend to cook a lamb leg for a long time or want to chop it into smaller pieces, you'll need to ask your butcher to remove all the fat and the skin.

### NEUTRAL OIL

The recipes often suggest using neutral oil, which is an oil with a mild flavor that won't overpower the rest of the mixture. These oils are generally grapeseed, canola, sunflower or peanut. Nonetheless, it is recommended to taste the oil before using a large amount, because sometimes, especially with organic oils, an oil that is considered neutral can have a strong taste.

### RAS EL HANOUT

It's also a good idea to choose a ras el hanout by tasting several because the combination of spices varies greatly among producers. Look for it in Middle Eastern and specialty food stores.

### SAFFRON

Saffron is a very special spice and fairly common in North African recipes. It can be disappointing, however, if it's not good quality (good saffron is very expensive). If you're not sure how to use it, it's better to substitute another spice of your choice: ginger, allspice, turmeric (which tints food like saffron does), ras el hanout, etc. All work well in meat dishes.

### SUMAC

Sumac (an acidic, red spice), as well as za'atar (a mixture of spices that includes za'atar itself (similar to thyme), sumac, roasted sesame seeds and salt), are the only spices used in this book that are not found in supermarkets.

### TAGINE

The tagine is a North African dish made of glazed clay with a conical lid that seals perfectly. This tool helps cook foods at a very low temperature and with little liquid. The cooked foods are very tender, and the sauce, made primarily from the water contained in the ingredients, is very flavorful. The disadvantage of this type of cooking is the time. Designed to be used over embers, tagines break when used over high heat, so the cooking times are very long. This is why, in Western kitchens, it's preferable to start the recipes in a skillet or sauté pan. You can thus precook the foods and flavor them by browning in fat. You can then transfer the contents to the tagine and continue cooking over low heat. If you don't have a tagine, you can continue to use the skillet, covering it and finishing the cooking over low heat. The advantage of the "completely in the skillet" method is that you can quickly reduce a sauce that is too thin at the end of cooking by increasing the temperature of the burner.

### TAHINI

Tahini is sesame paste, but it is more like a cream than a paste. It must be mixed well to give it a uniform texture before using. It's often used thinned, and, to ensure its texture remains smooth once it's mixed into a liquid (such as water or lemon juice), it must be added to and mixed into the liquid gradually. Tahini can be found in the international foods aisle of large supermarkets, Middle Eastern food stores and health food stores.

### TOMATOES

Tomatoes are widely used in Middle Eastern cooking, but their flavor is often disappointing if they are not in season. If a recipe calls for raw tomatoes but they're out of season, I often suggest using cherry or grape tomatoes instead. While cooking, tomatoes will generally absorb the flavors of the dish and lose a little of their moistness, which makes them tastier. However, in recipes in which they are cooked to flavor a stock or soup (for example, in couscous stock or Harira), I recommend using tomato paste instead of out-of-season tomatoes; 1 tablespoon (15 ml) tomato paste easily replaces 4 tomatoes.

### ZEST

To zest a citrus fruit is to remove the colored and scented outter peel using a zester or vegetable peeler. These tools help to separate the peel from the pith, the whitish and bitter part between the flesh and the peel. If you also want to juice the fruit, you need to zest it first. It's best to choose citrus fruits that are untreated after harvesting or organically grown for zesting.

# LEBANESE

# IRANIAN

# GREEK AND TURKISH

| | | | |
|---|---|---|---|
| 1 | Greek Salad (Horiatiki Salata) ............... 17<br>Taramosalata............................... 7 | 2 | Tahini Soup (Tahinosoupa).................... 27 |
| 3 | Rice Pilaf................................34 | 4 | Moussaka ................................. 48<br>Shish Kebab ................................ 50 |
| 5 | Pollock with Tarator Sauce ................... 52<br>(Tajen Samak bi Tahini) | 6 | Baklava.................................... 60<br>Date & Walnut Cake ........................ 67<br>Turkish Delight............................ 61 |

# MOROCCAN AND TUNISIAN

| | | | |
|---|---|---|---|
| 1 | Chakchouka Ragout ......................... 21<br>Mechouia Salad ............................ 18<br>Oven-Roasted Tomato Petals ............... 20<br>Slata Jida................................. 22<br>Tunisian Sandwiches......................... 13 | 2 | Harira (Ramada Soup)........................26<br>Tomato & Garlic Soup........................ 25 |
| 3 | Couscous............................... 30 | 4 | Chicken & Almond Tagine .................... 41<br>Chicken Bastilla .............................. 49<br>Chicken Couscous ...........................38<br>Chicken with Olives & Lemons.............. 43<br>Koftas (Meatballs) & Eggs.................... 44<br>Lamb & Apricot Tagine.......................39<br>Lamb & Prune Tagine ....................... 40<br>Roasted Lamb (Mrouzia)..................... 46<br>Seven-Vegetable Couscous ................... 37 |
| 5 | Fish Bastilla.................................. 55<br>Fish with Chermoula Sauce...................56<br>Monkfish Tagine ............................54 | 6 | Almond Briouats (Pastry Triangles)...........62<br>Custard Bastilla..............................66<br>Gazelle Horns ............................... 63<br>Ghorayebah................................. 65<br>Glazed Oranges ............................ 69<br>Mint Tea ....................................58 |

# TABLE OF CONTENTS

# 1

## APPETIZERS

# 2

## SOUPS & SAUCES

# 3

## SIDE DISHES

# 4

## MEATS

# 5

## FISH

# 6

## DESSERTS

# INDEX OF RECIPES

# THEMATIC INDEX

## ACKNOWLEDGMENTS

Thanks to Emmanuel Le Vallois and Rose-Marie Domenico for renewing their trust in me for this book.

Thanks to Audrey Génin for leading this project with kindness and talent.

Thanks to Sonia and Fred Lucano for their work: beautiful as always!

Thanks to Sousan Majidi for introducing me to Iranian cooking; to Linda Abraham and Suzy Saadia for the warm demonstration of Lebanese cooking; to Narjiss Charef for their helpful advice on Moroccan cooking; and to Madame Sadadou for instilling in me a love of couscous at an early age!

Thanks to my sister, Julia, for her encouragement since the start of my culinary adventures.

Thanks to Julie Andrieu for helping me live my passion.

And to Jérôme, a huge thank you.


Thanks to Emery & cie for the paints (www.emeryetcie.com).